Hocking Hills Hiking Tra

*A Guide to the Hiking
Trails of the Hocking Hills*

ISBN-13: 978-1-940087-58-0

About the author:

Jannette Quackenbush is the author of 30 books, including hiking trails of the Appalachian Region and the Hocking Hills. She is a veteran hiker, a seasoned backpacker, and a career author/naturalist/ travel guide who resides in the Hocking Hills and hikes all these trails regularly.

Cover image: Ash Cave, Kenneth Keifer

Interior Images: Jannette Quackenbush

Like this book? Check out Jannette's

Ohio Hiking Trails

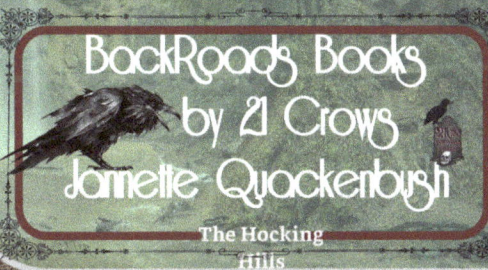

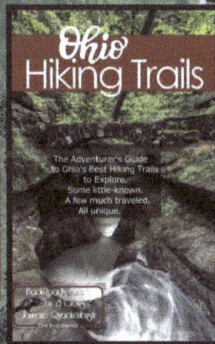

Ohio
Hiking Trails

The Adventurer's Guide
to Ohio's Best Hiking Trails
to Explore.
Some little-known.
A few much traveled.
All unique.

BackRoads Books
by 21 Crows
Jannette Quackenbush

**The Hocking
Hills**

Table of Contents

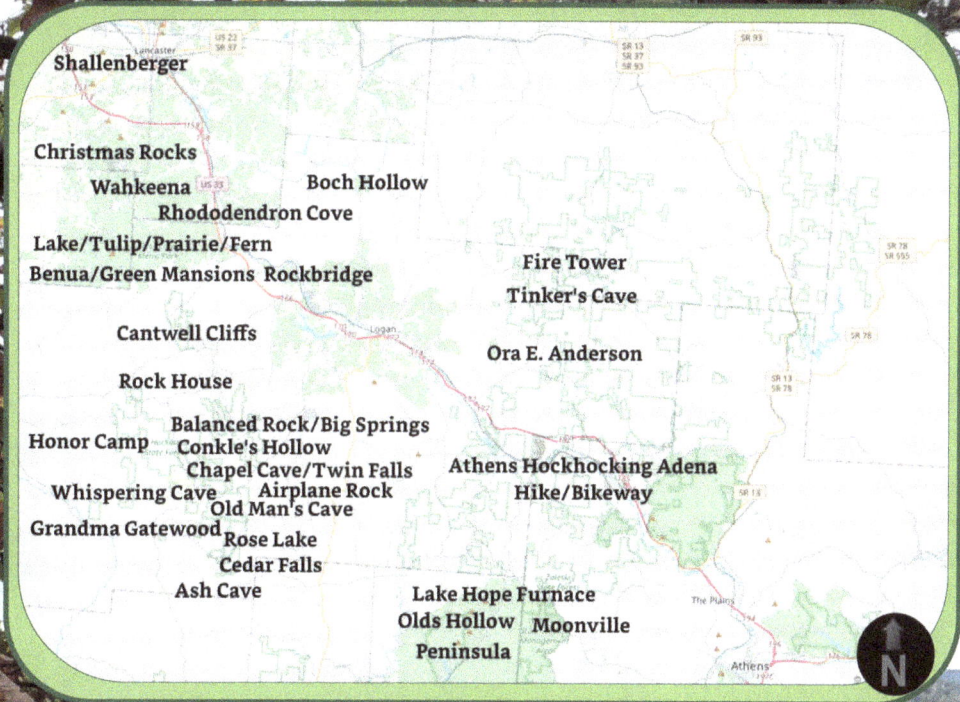

Shallenberger

Christmas Rocks
Wahkeena   Boch Hollow
     Rhododendron Cove
Lake/Tulip/Prairie/Fern
Benua/Green Mansions Rockbridge
                              Fire Tower
                              Tinker's Cave
     Cantwell Cliffs
                         Ora E. Anderson
     Rock House

     Balanced Rock/Big Springs
Honor Camp   Conkle's Hollow
     Chapel Cave/Twin Falls   Athens Hockhocking Adena
Whispering Cave   Airplane Rock   Hike/Bikeway
         Old Man's Cave
Grandma Gatewood
         Rose Lake
         Cedar Falls
     Ash Cave
                    Lake Hope Furnace
               Olds Hollow Moonville
               Peninsula

N

These features are used on the trail description charts:

Quality of Trails:

Developed Trails—Man-made paths wide enough to comfortably hike with grass and brush typically removed. Features are usually added, such as steps, ramps, and bridges. They require routine maintenance.

Multi-use Trail—Used by pedestrians but may also be used by bikers and horseback riders.

Backcountry Trail—Not maintained and usually have no features like restrooms or camping facilities. Typically only used by experienced hikers.

Nature Trail—Routinely maintained and usually offer interpretive signs along the path.

Trail Road—Unpaved lane or road that vehicles may use.

Rail-trail—A paved or graveled trail made from an abandoned railroad corridor/track.

Types of Trails:

Out-and-Back—Begin and end at the same location, returning along the same route. Typically day hike trails.

Loop—Begin and end at the same location, but follow a trail/trails that form a loop. Typically day hike trails.

Point-to-Point—Begin and end in different locations, usually for long-distance, extended trips for backpacking. Typically multiple-day hiking like the Appalachian Trail.

One-Way—Trails maintained in a loop and developed, for the safety of the natural area and hikers, so that hikers can only go one way from start to finish, unable to turn to go in the opposite direction. Often seen in cliff areas where it is unsafe to pass or areas with protected wildlife species/plants to maintain minimal human interference.

Spur—Path that branches off a main trail and leads to a dead end, usually at a point of interest such as an overlook or historical feature.

Elements to Heed When Hiking

- Most of the trails in this book are easy to follow and well-marked. Still, note your starting location on your positioning/ mapping devices before your hike so you can retrace your steps if you get lost.

- Leave an itinerary of your travel destinations with someone before you depart.

- Bear share the same paths as humans. Although not often, I have seen bear near the trails in this book. I kept my distance and gave them the right of way, talking to myself so as not to startle them. Be aware of your surroundings so you do not stumble into their path and surprise them. But also be conscious of the fact that they may sense you long before you realize they are there. Carry a light source so that if your journey lasts into the dark, you can light the path.

- Snakes, spiders, and other creatures (that fall into the category that some people might find menacing) live in these natural areas. Most you will never see because you are a huge, scary predator to them, and they simply want to be left alone. You are in their house and backyard, so respect them and veer from their path. Leave them alone.

- It is noted if pets/dogs are typically allowed on a specific trail. However, check for updates before taking your pet with you on a trip or hike.

- Most parks in this book require hikers to stay on the trail proper due to dangerous cliffs and the protection of rare plants and animals. This includes no swimming or wading in creeks or waterways.

Map Notations:

Notes hiking trail route. Black arrows usually show trails without color blazes. Colored arrows typically reflect color of blazes or colors on trail maps at the location, although blaze color may be changed on a trail over time.

Hiking trail note or location point.

A Little Bit about GPS Coordinates and QR Codes Used in the Book—

Using GPS tracking and a very basic way to use tracking on your desktop or phone:

Roads, trails, and hiking locations are often remote and do not have a street number or name. I use GPS because the two numbers given, called coordinates, uniquely identify a precise location. Hikers can enter coordinates by typing or copying and pasting them into the search box of a mapping app and clicking the "search" button (magnifying glass). The location will display with a red pin on the map and details (if available) on the left. If directions are needed, an origin can be added with a simple click of the "directions" button, which will pull up a box so a starting point can be typed.

Here are the coordinates for the town of Moonville: 39.308828, -82.324810

A minus sign before the second number indicates that the location is *west* of the prime meridian. If a minus sign is located in front of the first number, it will show degrees *south* of the equator.

If that flew right over your head, no big deal. Just understand that it is important that the *minus sign* is with the correct number because the placement of the minus sign is crucial. Do not confuse the two and accidentally get them backward because this specific coordinate -39.308828, 82.324810 (noting the minus sign is in the first number this time) will take you to the center of the Indian Ocean and 250 miles from the closest land!

In this book, I use QR Codes as an easy way to share the hiking trailhead/parking area with readers who can pull the route up on their phone and get an idea of their destination. It can be picked up in almost any mapping system and take travelers to the area. QR Codes, mapping systems, and courses are not perfect. Areas change, and sometimes, a newer, better course is available. Always route your origin and destination before leaving for a particular trip, check for trail closures and revisions, and ensure the route is safe. Also note that some areas in the Hocking Hills Region do not have functional cell phone service. You may have difficulties setting up your *return* route so make sure you map a round trip.

How to use QR Codes: Hold your smartphone camera app to the QR code as if taking a picture and allow it to focus in the viewfinder. The phone will recognize the code as you move it toward the QR code (you may have to move it back and forth slowly a few times to get the camera to focus). When you see your mapping app name show up, touch it, and the map will show up in your mapping system.

A Note about using QR codes for the trails in this book:

Do not rely on the app's hiking system so much that you follow it off a cliff. It does not have a conscience or a sense of right or wrong. And it certainly does not have an IQ, so no matter how many apps you have on the phone, you are still smarter than all of them. So do not rely solely on your phone and the maps. Use your judgment first.

Birds of Prey hikers see near the trails in the Hocking Hills

Barred Owl

Great Horned Owl

Screech Owl

Red-tailed Hawk

Turkey Vulture

Bald Eagle

Mammals hikers see along the trails in the Hocking Hills

White-tailed Deer

Eastern Cottontail

Chipmunk

Raccoon

Opossum

Bobcat

Skunk

Red Fox

Coyote

Black Bear

Beaver

You may see baby animals, especially fawns, that appear to be alone. Please do not pick them up. Leave them. Their only defense mechanism is to be still and quiet where their mother left them if a possible predator, like yourself, comes close. Mama deer is nearby! She knows her size makes her stick out and to keep the baby from risk, she hides somewhere just out of sight. Quietly, walk away.

Common spring wildflowers hikers see near the trails in the Hocking Hills

Phlox

Spring Beauty

Bloodroot

Common Blue Violet

White Trillium

Purple Dead Nettle

Rue Anemone

Blue-eyed Mary

Fire Pink

Golden Ragwort

Ash Cave
Hocking Hills State
Park

Hocking Hills State Park & Hocking State Forest

Old Man's Cave

Rose Lake

Ash Cave

Cedar Falls

Grandma Gatewood

Conkle's Hollow

Whispering Cave

Cantwell Cliffs

Rock House

Honor Camp Trail

Cantwell Cliffs

Rock House

Honor Camp   Conkle's Hollow

Whispering Cave
                    Old Man's Cave
Grandma Gatewood   Rose Lake
                    Cedar Falls
            Ash Cave

Image: OpenStreetMap

Hocking Hills State Park
Old Man's Cave

Old Man's Cave is one of the major hiking trails of Hocking Hills State Park. Once also known as Dead Man's Cave, it was called such for the aged trapper named Retzler, who lived there from the mid to late 1700s and whose remains, along with his dog, Harper, and a gun, were discovered in the 1800s.

The cave is made up of a gritty, reddish sandstone called Black Hand Sandstone and was left behind more than 200 million years ago when the Appalachian Mountains uplifted out of an ancient ocean covering Ohio because of the shifting of the earth's crust. As the ocean drained from the mountains, it left behind hills made of massive piles of sand, rock, and gravel. Along with these changes, water and erosion carved out the gorge of the cave to form the deep pocket, cracks, and grooves.

Parking/Trailhead:

Hocking Hills State Park
Old Man's Cave Parking/Trailhead
State Route 664
Logan, Ohio 43138
(39.436394, -82.539169)

Hike: The one-way loop trail is approximately 1.0 to 1.5 miles long and begins at the wooden kiosk at Upper Falls and ends at the Visitor Center. Hikers must stay on trail.

Type of Trail:	Quality:	Markings:
Loop	*Nature Trail *Dirt path with steps/bridges/ high cliffs	Blue: Bottom of Gorge (Blue Blazes on Trees) Red: Top of the Gorge Rim Trail (Red Blazes)
Distance:	**Access:**	**Wheelchair Access:**
1.0 to 1.5 miles Heavy Use. Plan an early morning weekday trip.	*Open dawn to dusk/365 days a year. *Well-behaved dogs on leash allowed. Cliffs.	Not in the gorge (Wheelchair accessibility begins near the Camp Office, past Visitor Center, and to Lodge Road)
Restrooms:	**Features:**	**Parking GPS:**
Yes, Visitor Center	Cliffs, Waterfalls, Rock Formations	39.436394, -82.539169

Hikers can choose from 2 exits:

Exit 1—At Old Man's Cave, which ends at the Naturalist Cabin and Visitor Center. **The trail is 1.0 miles and takes about 60 minutes.**

Exit 2— Past Old Man's Cave to Lower Falls, following a steep incline with an elevation change at the winding stairway, which ends at the Naturalist Cabin and Visitor Center. **Exit 2 is 1.5 miles and takes about 1.5 hours.**
-Hikers can also take a spur trail to Broken Rock Falls, which is 0.25 miles in and 0.25 miles out and is a two-way trail.
-Hikers can also access a trail near the **A-Frame Bridge** by the Naturalist Cabin to head to Cedar Falls and Ash Cave. It is a 6.0-miles hike one-way to Ash Cave, and there is no bus service for return hikers. **Takes about 5 to 7 hours.**
-A **wheelchair/stroller accessible** trail runs from the Park/Camp office past the visitor center to Lodge Road. It is a little more than 0.5 miles in length and includes a ramp and observation deck at Upper Falls.
-For a strenuous extended walk, hikers can take the Blue Blaze TRAIL to Lower Falls, past Rose Lake, the Cedar Falls A-Frame Bridge, and then to Cedar Falls, which is 3.0 more miles, one way.
Interesting sights include: Devil's Bathtub and Sphinx Head.

Old Man's Cave Trail Map

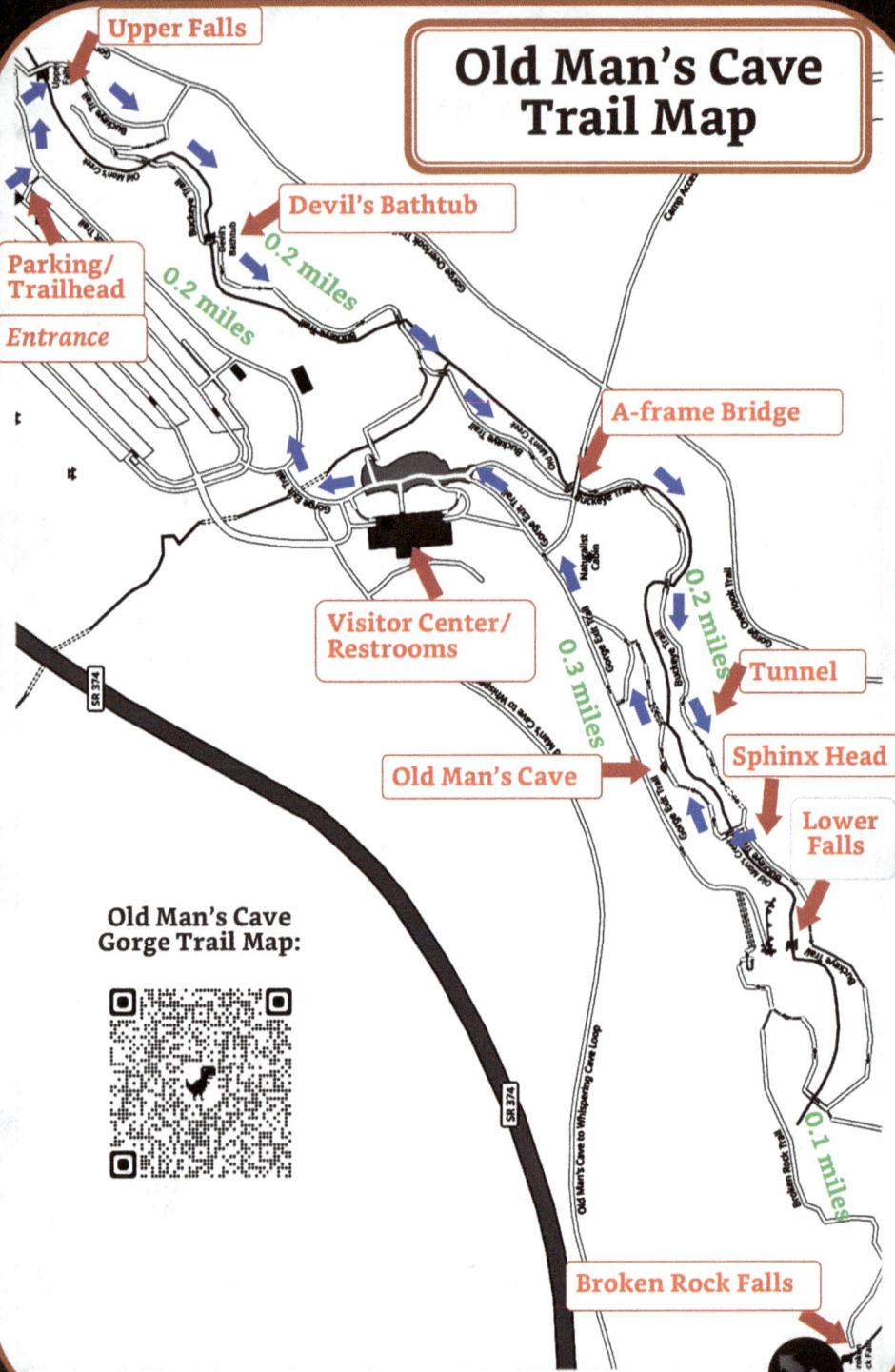

Upper Falls

Devil's Bathtub

0.2 miles

0.2 miles

Parking/ Trailhead

Entrance

A-frame Bridge

Visitor Center/ Restrooms

0.2 miles

Tunnel

0.3 miles

Sphinx Head

Old Man's Cave

Lower Falls

SR 374

Old Man's Cave Gorge Trail Map:

0.1 miles

Broken Rock Falls

100 m
500 ft

Image: OpenStreet Map CyclOSM

N

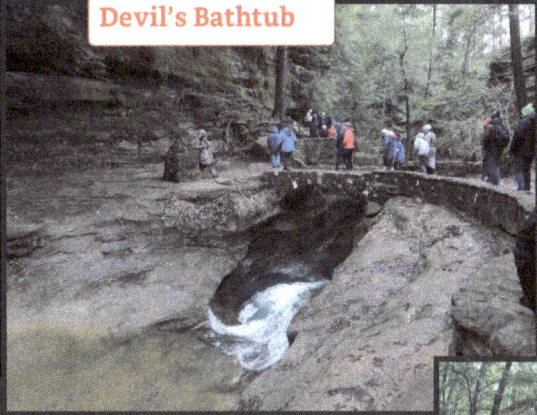
Devil's Bathtub

Upper Falls

Tunnel

A-frame Bridge, above

Lower Falls

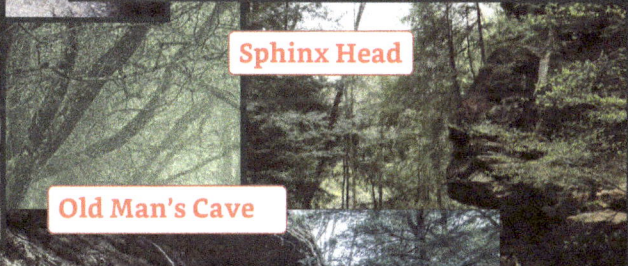
Sphinx Head

Old Man's Cave

Broken Rock Falls

Hocking Hills State Park
Rose Lake

Long ago, it was just a little valley belonging to the Iles family. After the State of Ohio procured the land around it, they dammed the creek to form an artificial lake, calling the valley around it Rose Hollow and the reservoir Rose Lake. It is just below the campground and stocked with fish.

The calm waters also have tiny translucent, bell-shaped freshwater jellyfish about nickel size.

Parking/Trailhead:

Hocking Hills State Park
Rose Lake Fisherman Pull-off
State Route 374
Logan, Ohio 43138
(39.432160, -82.528120)

Hike: An out and back spur trail through
the forest to Rose Lake and then a loop trail around the small reservoir. Hikers must stay on trail.

Type of Trail:	Quality:	Markings:
-Out and Back *(spur to Lake Trail)* -**Loop** *(Lake Trail)*	*Developed dirt path with muddy spots and may have to get feet wet across shallow creeks.	**Red**: Should be red blazes from the parking lot to the lake, however, the blazes are almost too worn to see. No blazes or signage for lake loop. **Trail Start/End for loop: 39.429212, -82.535325**
Distance:	**Access:**	**Wheelchair Access:**
Hike from fisherman's lot to Rose Lake-0.5 miles, one-way Rose Lake Loop: 1.2 miles Takes about 1.5 hours to hike.	*Open dawn to dusk/365 days a year. *Well-behaved dogs on leash allowed.	No
Restrooms:	**Features:**	**Parking GPS:**
No	Lake, forest	39.432160, -82.528120 Lot is very small.

Hikers start at the Fisherman's Parking Access on State Route 374 between Cedar Falls and the Hocking Hills Walk-in Campground and must cross State Route 374. It is marked across the road. The spur trail is through a forest and dips downward to Rose Lake. When reaching the lake and loop trail, hikers should mark this entrance/exit as there are many outlaw spur trails and the trail blazes are worn so it is difficult to find the loop trailhead/spur for the return to the parking lot. The trail loops around the lake through woodland and across some small creeks.
Interesting sights include: A bird blind along the trail for bird viewing and freshwater jellyfish in the cool water.

Rose Lake Trail Map

Parking/ Trailhead

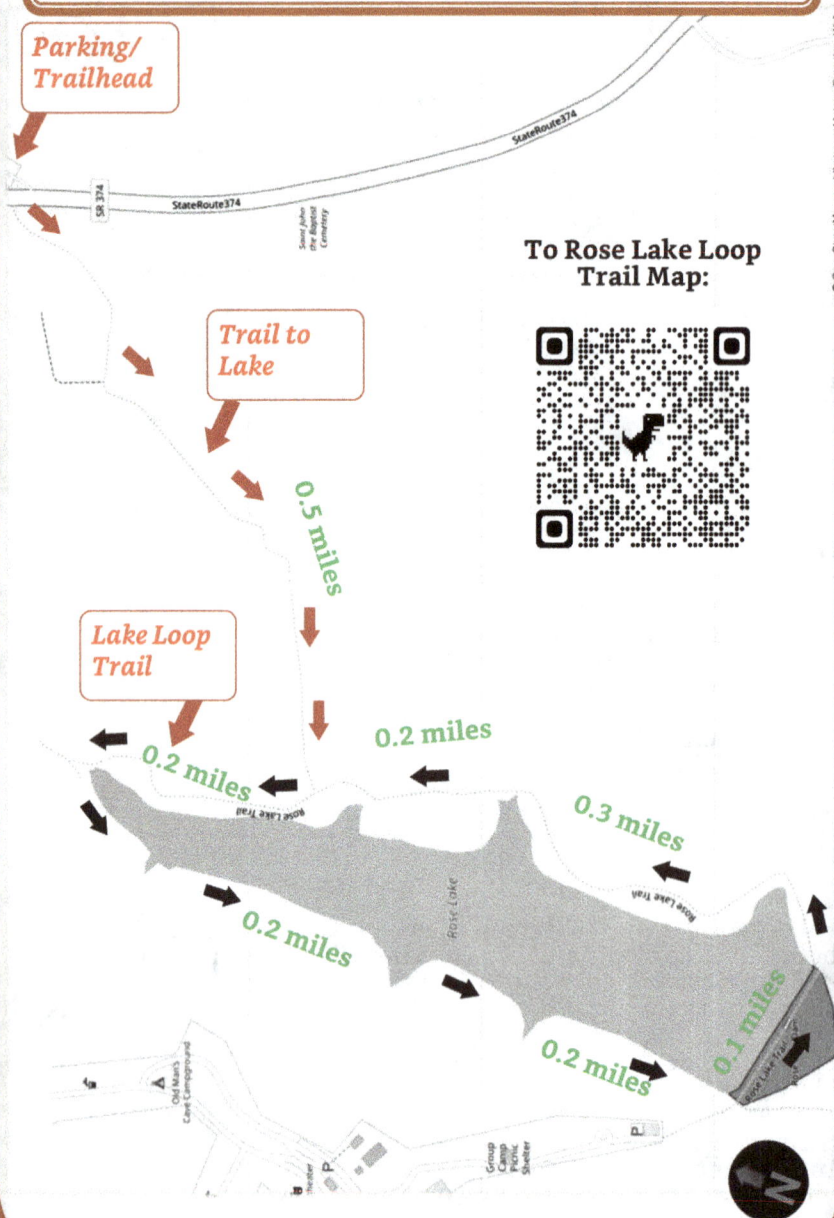

StateRoute374

SR 374

StateRoute374

Saint John the Baptist Cemetery

Trail to Lake

To Rose Lake Loop Trail Map:

0.5 miles

Lake Loop Trail

0.2 miles

0.2 miles

0.2 miles

0.3 miles

Rose Lake Trail

0.2 miles

Rose Lake

Rose Lake Trail

0.2 miles

0.1 miles

Rose Lake Trail

Old Man's Cave Campground

Group Camp Picnic Shelter

P

P

N

100 m
500 ft

Trailhead

Fishing at lake

Along out and back trail to lake

During Annual Winter Hike

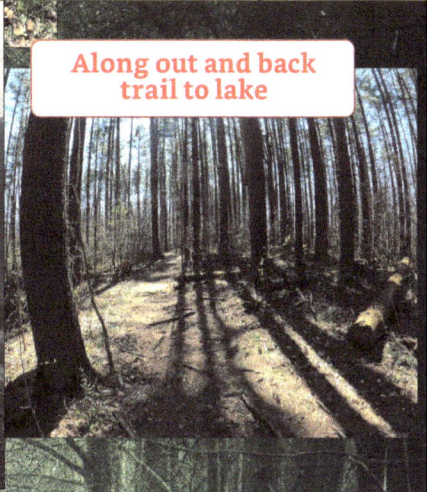

Hocking Hills State Park
Ash Cave

Pulpit Rock

Ashes

Ash Cave is one of the major hiking trails of Hocking Hills State Park. In the 1800s, archeologists and artifact collectors discovered mounds of wood ashes, human remains, and pottery within this large recess cave, presumed to come from its ancient habitation. Such, it was dubbed "Ash Cave." Although these ashes are all but gone today, hikers can see remnants scattered in layers of packed sand beneath the large stone boulder at the end of the concrete path as they enter the hollow. In the 1800s, pioneers also took shelter within the cave, and later, as the area became more heavily settled, local congregations held church meetings here. When entering the cave, look to the right and behold the flat stone where preachers stood to deliver sermons to their flock. Ash Cave's natural auditorium shape offered good acoustics—sound range and quality. This stone was known as Preachers Rock or Pulpit Rock. Ash Cave's waterfall is 83 feet.

Parking/Trailhead:

Hocking Hills State Park
Ash Cave Parking/Trailhead:
26400 OH-56
South Bloomingville, Ohio 43152
(39.395895, -82.545587)

Hike: The one-way loop trail is approximately 0.5 miles long and begins at the wooden kiosk near the parking lot. Hikers must stay on the trail. (39.396300, -82.545549) Wheelchair accessible to cave.

Type of Trail:	Quality:	Markings:
Loop	*Nature Trail *Mix of asphalt and dirt path with steps/bridges	Yellow: Ash Cave Trail (Yellow Blazes on Trees) Blue: Grandma Gatewood Trail
Distance:	**Access:**	**Wheelchair Access:**
0.5 miles. About 40 minutes to hike. Heavy Use. Plan a weekday trip. Hike early morning.	*Open dawn to dusk/365 days a year. *Well-behaved dogs on leash allowed.	Yes, there is a concrete path to the recess cave
Restrooms:	**Features:**	**Parking GPS:**
Yes, at parking lot and trail entrance	Cliffs, Waterfalls, Rock Formations	39.395895, -82.545587

The trail is approximately 0.5 miles long and takes about 40 minutes to hike. It is a one-way trail system to protect the delicate ecosystem, but it is wheelchair accessible (to a series of steps that are a strenuous climb). Wheelchairs can return as an out and back.

Hikers trek a concrete trail through a beautiful gorge with stately hemlocks and cliff walls. Halfway, there is a recess cave and a seasonal waterfall.

After reaching the cave/waterfall area, hikers (barring wheelchair users) must continue on the one-way trail system and up a series of steps to the rim trail, which leads (if turning right) back along the rim to the parking lot. Hikers can also turn left at the top of the steps for 2.3 miles one-way to Cedar Falls. The path is marked with signs.

Interesting sights include Pulpit Rock, and although it is illegal to carve on the wall today, early visitors left their mark on the stone. You can view their etchings from more than a hundred years ago. Pigeons also roost near the ceiling; you can hear their coos on quiet days.

Ash Cave Trail Map

Ash Cave Loop Trail Map:

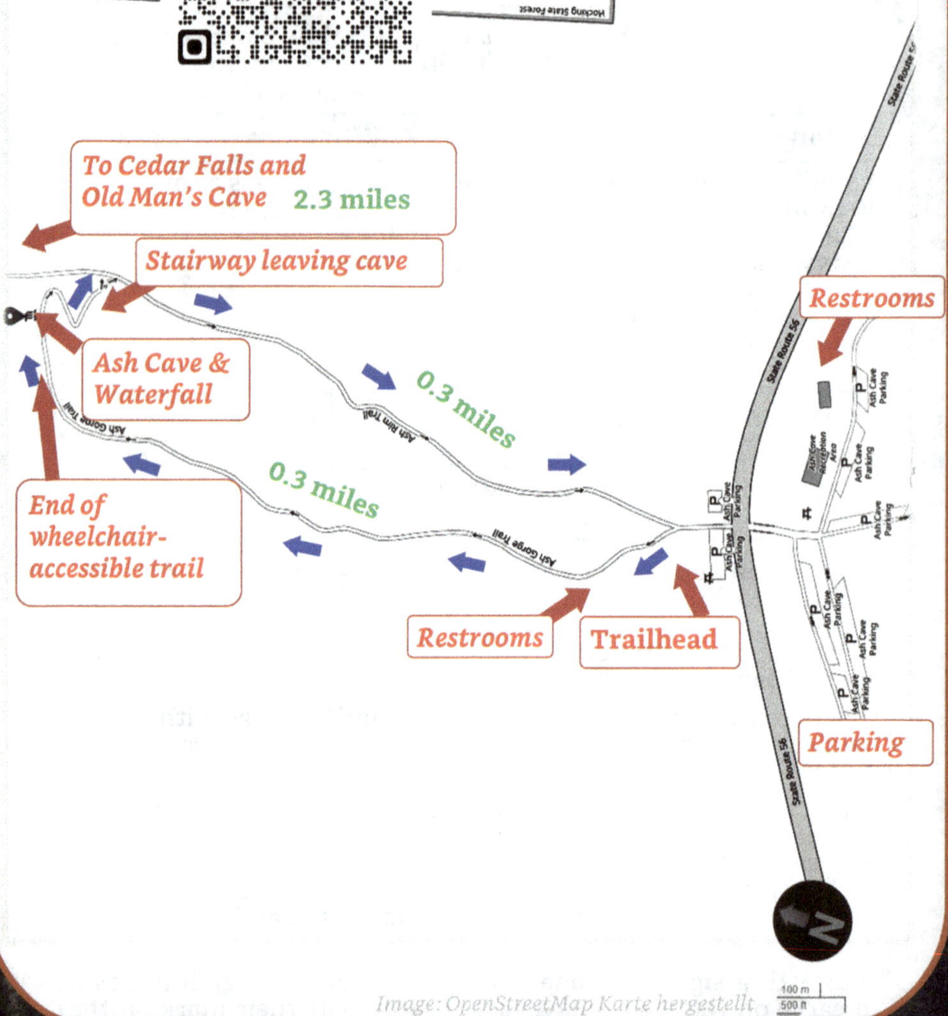
Hocking State Forest
To Cedar Falls and Old Man's Cave 2.3 miles
Stairway leaving cave
Ash Cave & Waterfall
End of wheelchair-accessible trail
0.3 miles
0.3 miles
Ash Rim Trail
Ash Gorge Trail
Restrooms
Trailhead
Restrooms
Parking
State Route 56
Ash Cave Parking
Ash Cave Recreation Area
100 m
500 ft

Image: OpenStreetMap Karte hergestellt

Winter in Ash Cave

Trail to Ash Cave

Stairway leaving
the cave

Hocking Hills State Park
Cedar Falls

Cedar Falls is one of the major hiking trails of Hocking Hills State Park. It is through the area of Cedar Falls that Shawnee and Delaware had a much-used path to cross the rugged terrain. There was once a massive beech tree along a darker section of the trace at the top of the falls with words engraved deeply into its ancient trunk, "This is the road to hell, 1782." It was passed down that in the 1700s, Shawnee marched their captives along this point, and one such doomed prisoner left the carving on the tree.

As pioneers began to settle the area, they misidentified the hemlock trees growing in the hills and valleys as cedar trees. So as they came upon Queer Creek and the waterfall made from its swift current flowing down the cliff, they named the cascading water Cedar Falls. Later, a grist mill once ran above the waterfall, employing the swift and powerful current of the water to run the wheel.

Parking/Trailhead:

Hocking Hills State Park
Cedar Falls Parking/Trailhead
21724 Ohio 374 Scenic
Logan, Ohio 43138
(39.418273, -82.526310)

Hike: The one-way loop trail is approximately 0.5 miles long and begins at the wooden kiosk at Cedar Falls Parking Area. Hikers must stay on trail.

Type of Trail:	Quality:	Markings:
Loop	*Developed Trail *Dirt path with steps/bridges	Yellow: Cedar Falls (Yellow Blazes on Trees) Red: Top of the Gorge Rim Trail (Red Blazes)
Distance:	**Access:**	**Wheelchair Access:**
0.5 miles, 40 minutes to hike. Heavy Use. Plan a weekday trip. Hike early morning.	*Open dawn to dusk/365 days a year. *Well-behaved dogs on leash allowed. Cliffs.	No
Restrooms:	**Features:**	**Parking GPS:**
Yes, at parking area	Cliffs, Waterfall, Rock Formations	39.418273, -82.526310

The path is approximately 0.5 miles long and relatively strenuous with steps. It is a one-way trail system with a waterfall, bridges, and unique rock formations. Halfway, hikers can take in the beauty of a seasonal waterfall reached by hiking a rugged trail down steps and along a dirt path. After getting to the waterfall area, hikers continue along the one-way trail system through rock formations, a boardwalk, and up a series of steps. The trail is marked with signs.

It takes approximately 40 minutes to hike the trail.

For a longer stretch of 2.2 miles, one-way, hikers can continue up a set of steps along the Gorge Overlook Trail to Old Man's Cave. It is marked with a metal map and wooden signs and continues past the A-frame bridge at the top of Cedar Falls.

Interesting sights include: Watch in the creek along the trail near Cedar Falls for the large, resident snapping turtles basking near the water's surface.

Cedar Falls Trail Map

A-frame Bridge

Cedar Falls Loop Trail Map:

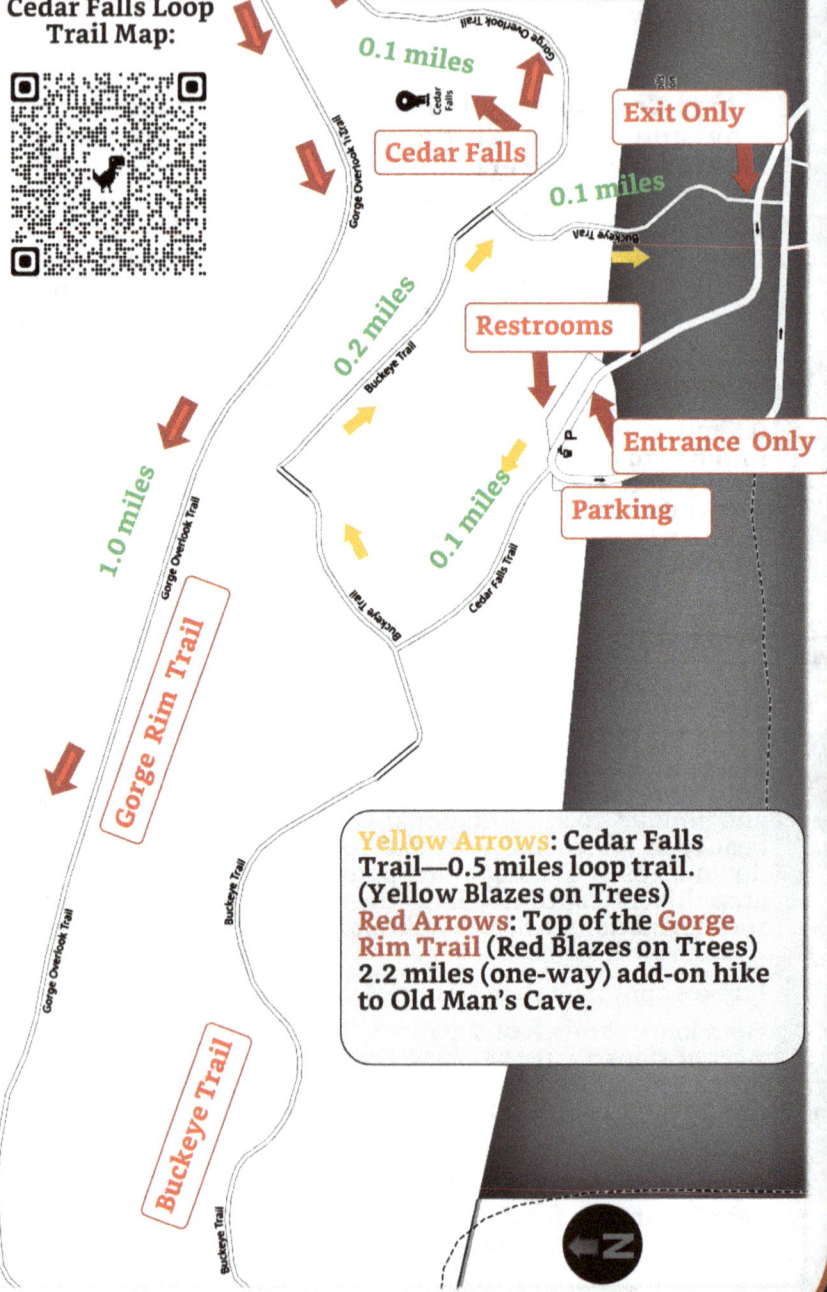

0.1 miles

Gorge Overlook Trail

Cedar Falls

Cedar Falls

Exit Only

0.1 miles

Buckeye Trail

0.2 miles

Buckeye Trail

Restrooms

Entrance Only

1.0 miles

Gorge Overlook Trail

0.1 miles

Buckeye Trail

Cedar Falls Trail

Parking

Gorge Rim Trail

Yellow Arrows: Cedar Falls Trail—0.5 miles loop trail. (Yellow Blazes on Trees)
Red Arrows: Top of the **Gorge Rim Trail** (Red Blazes on Trees) 2.2 miles (one-way) add-on hike to Old Man's Cave.

Gorge Overlook Trail

Buckeye Trail

Buckeye Trail

Buckeye Trail

N

100 m
500 ft

Image: OpenStreetMap Karte hergestellt aus

First stretch of trail

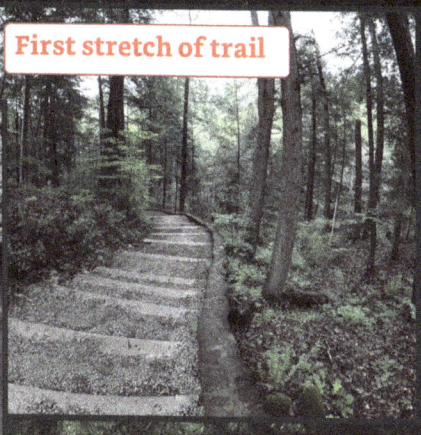
Marked with yellow tree blazes

Cedar Falls

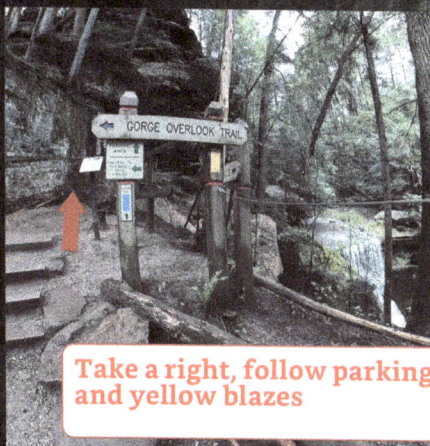
Take a right, follow parking sign and yellow blazes

Boardwalk through rock formations

Hikers can also take the steps to view the A-frame Bridge

Hocking Hills State Park
Grandma Gatewood

Hocking Hills State Park is home to the Grandma Gatewood Hiking Trail, honoring Emma Gatewood, an Ohio hiking pioneer. Gatewood endured many hardships and hiked the 2,168-mile Appalachian Trail alone, inspiring many others to overcome great odds. The Grandma Gatewood Hiking Trail covers several of the main hiking areas in the park – Old Man's Cave, Cedar Falls, and Ash Cave.

Parking/Trailhead:

Hocking Hills State Park
Old Man's Cave Parking/Trailhead
State Route 664
Logan, Ohio 43138
(39.436394, -82.539169)

Hike: Out and back trail covering several major hiking spots including Old Man's Cave, Ash Cave, and Cedar Falls. Hikers must stay on trail.

Type of Trail:	Quality:	Markings:
Out and Back	*Nature Trail *Dirt path with steps/bridges/cliffs	**Blue**: Bottom of Gorge (Blue Blazes on Trees)

Distance:	Access:	Wheelchair Access:
5.0 miles one way. Total 10.0 miles within park. Heavy Use. Plan a weekday trip. Hike early morning.	*Open dawn to dusk/365 days a year. *Well-behaved dogs on leash allowed. Cliffs.	No

Restrooms:	Features:	Parking GPS:
Yes, Visitor Center/Ash Cave/Cedar Falls	Cliffs, Waterfalls, Rock Formations	39.436394, -82.539169

Hikers follow the gorge from Upper Falls at Old Man's Cave through Cedar Falls and then to Ash Cave. Hike is considered strenuous.

Interesting sights include: The Grandma Gatewood Hiking Trail follows the blue blazes of the Buckeye Trail through the park, passing many of the famous landmarks of Hocking Hills State Park:

In Old Man's Cave: Devil's Bathtub, Sphinx Head, and Old Man's Cave.

Cedar Falls: The A-frame bridge and waterfall at Cedar Falls.

Ash Cave: The waterfall at Ash Cave.

Grandma Gatewood Trail Map

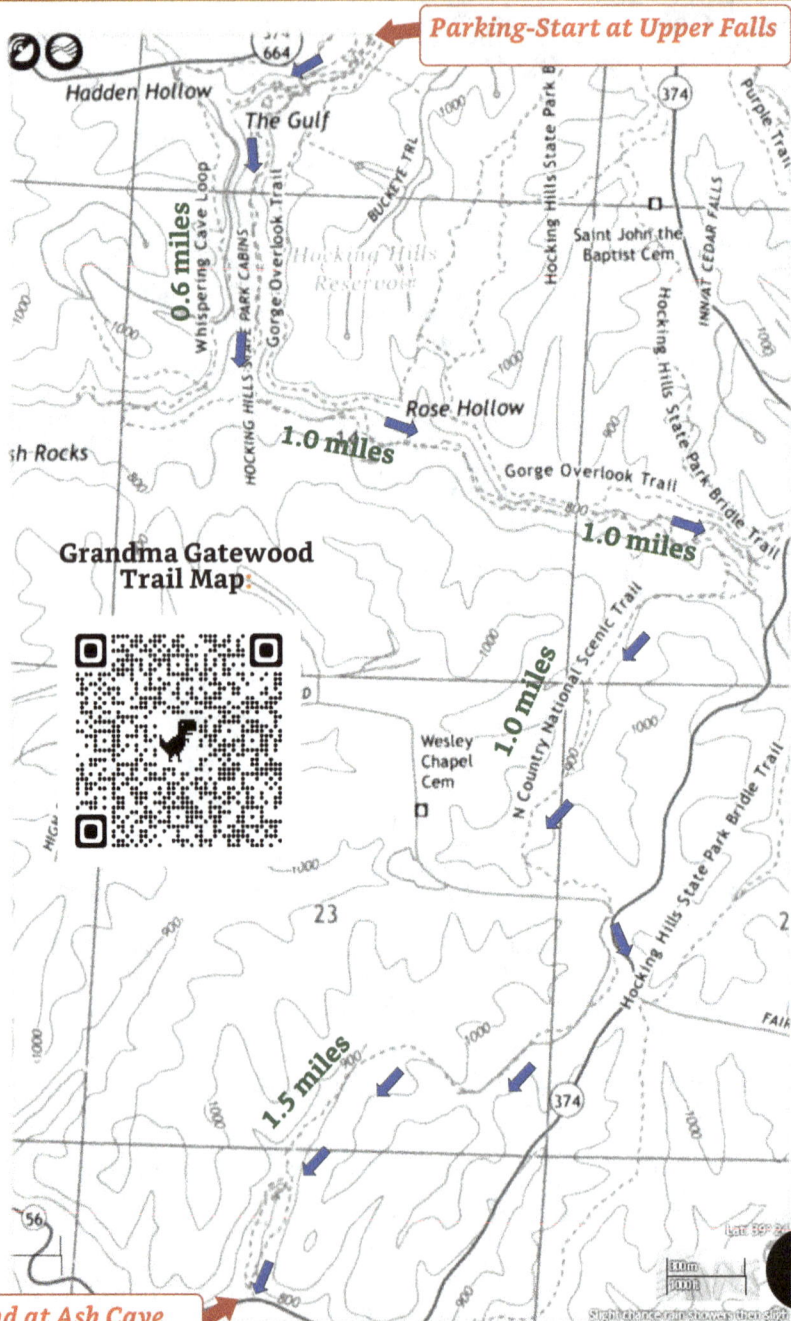

Hadden Hollow

The Gulf

374
664

Whispering Cave Loop

0.6 miles

HOCKING HILLS STATE PARK CABINS

Gorge Overlook Trail

BUCKEYE TRL

Hocking Hills Reservoir

Hocking Hills State Park B

374

Purple Trail

INN AT CEDAR FALLS

Saint John the Baptist Cem

Hocking Hills State Park Bridle Trail

Rose Hollow

1.0 miles

sh Rocks

Gorge Overlook Trail

1.0 miles

Grandma Gatewood Trail Map:

N Country National Scenic Trail

1.0 miles

Wesley Chapel Cem

Hocking Hills State Park Bridle Trail

23

1.5 miles

374

FAIR

56

Lat 39° 2

100m

Slight chance rain showers then sligh

Old Man's Cave

OLD MAN'S CAVE

Cedar Falls

Ash Cave

Hocking Hills State Park
Conkle's Hollow

Conkle's Hollow is one of the major hiking trails of Hocking Hills State Park. Conkle's Hollow is a nature preserve with upper-rim and lower-gorge trails. The upper trail has scenic views, especially during the autumn leaf change. The lower trail is wheelchair-accessible and follows a gently flowing creek, waterfalls, and small recess caves.

This gorge has an age-old legend attached to it. When pioneers floated along the Ohio River searching for a place to settle, a band of Shawnees would ambush the boats and steal from the travelers. Learning about this trap, a group of settlers carrying a large pot of gold coins waylaid the Shawnee's ambush. The settlers chased the thieves into Conkle's Hollow, trapped the men in its dead-end, and murdered them. But not before the Shawnee hid the money somewhere within. No one has ever found the coins; some believe they are still there, along with the ghosts of the Shawnee who protect the ill-gotten treasure.

Parking/Trailhead:

Hocking Hills State Park
Conkle's Hollow State Nature Preserve
Trailhead/Parking
24858 Big Pine Road
Rockbridge, Ohio 43149
(39.453543, -82.573520)

Hike: Lower Gorge Trail is 0.75 miles, begins at parking lot. Out and back. Rim Trail is 2.5 miles one-way and loop. From the parking lot, follow along Lower Gorge Trail and turn at the wooden steps. Hikers must stay on trail.

Type of Trail:	Quality:	Markings:
-Lower Trail is an out and back. -Rim Trail is a Loop	*Nature Trail *Dirt path with steps/bridges/cliffs	**Green**: Bottom of Gorge (Green Blazes on Trees) **Red**: Top of the Gorge Rim Trail (Red Blazes)

Distance:	Access:	Wheelchair Access:
Lower: 0.5 miles –1 hour hike Rim: 1.9 miles-2-hour hike Heavy Use. Plan a weekday trip. Hike early morning.	*Open dawn to dusk/365 days a year. *No Pets Allowed	Lower gorge trail only.

Restrooms:	Features:	Parking GPS:
Yes, in parking lot	Cliffs, Waterfalls, Rock Formations	39.453543, -82.573520

There are 2 Trails to hike, Upper Rim Trail
and Lower Gorge Trail:

The Lower Gorge Trail is a 0.75 miles long, wheelchair-accessible trail on concrete. It takes about 1 hour to hike the trail. **Interesting sights include:** One small cave marked with a sign is Horsehead Grotto, whose name comes from a stone on the left side of the entrance shaped like a horse's head.

The Upper Rim Trail is a one-way trail that is 2.5 miles long. It involves a moderate to steep incline, steps, 70 to 100-foot cliff drops, paths with visible roots, uneven rocks, and steep terrain. It is not suitable for young children, unfit adults, or pets. **Interesting sights include:** Breathtaking views during autumn leaf changes in October.

Conkle's Hollow State Nature Preserve Trail Map

Conkle's Hollow Gorge Trail Map:

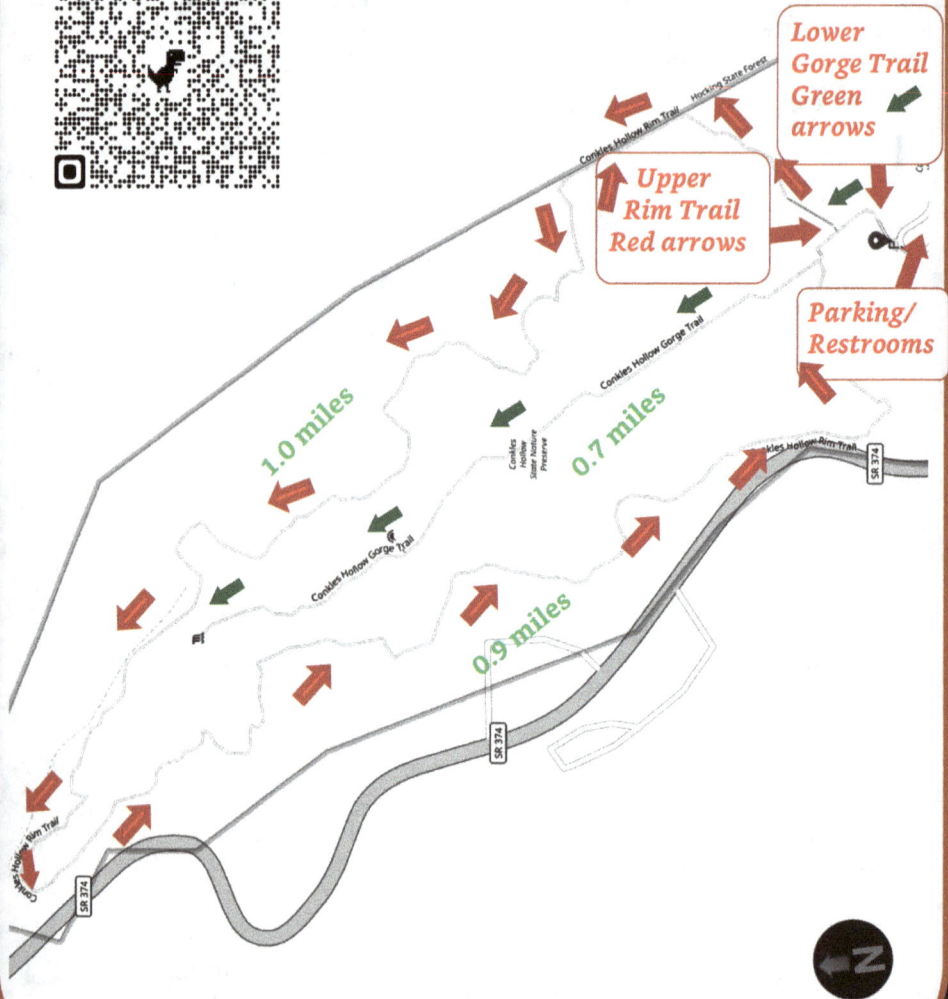

Lower Gorge Trail Green arrows

Upper Rim Trail Red arrows

Parking/ Restrooms

Conkles Hollow Rim Trail

Hocking State Forest

Conkles Hollow Gorge Trail

Conkles Hollow State Nature Preserve

Conkles Hollow Gorge Trail

1.0 miles

0.7 miles

0.9 miles

Conkles Hollow Rim Trail

SR 374

SR 374

SR 374

Conkles Hollow Rim Trail

N

Image: OpenStreetMap Karte hergestellt

100 m
500 ft

Conkle's Hollow Rim Trail in mid-October

Conkle's Lower Gorge Trail Horsehead Grotto

Horsehead

Hocking Hills State Park
Whispering Cave

Whispering Cave is one of the major hiking trails of Hocking Hills State Park. In days past, Whispering Cave was a more remote recess cave and a stopover for Paleo, Archaic, Hopewell, and Adena Peoples in their journeys. Some of these early dwellers left remnants of their stays behind, which, in the mid-1900s, were discovered, leading treasure hunters to excavate holes to remove the artifacts. Visitors with a keen eye can still see these illegally dug pits throughout the cave.

In the late 1800s and early 1900s, Whispering Cave was called Temple Chapel, and church-goers visited for religious meetings. Whispering Cave's waterfall is 79 feet.

Parking/Trailhead:

Hocking Hills State Park
Old Man's Cave Parking/Trailhead
Whispering Cave
State Route 664
Logan, Ohio 43138
(39.436394, -82.539169)

Hike: Park at Old Man's Cave to access the trail —it is a 5-mile, one-way loop. Hikers must go the entire 5.0 miles loop as it is one-way. Hikers must stay on trail.

Type of Trail:	Quality:	Markings:
Loop	*Nature Trail *Dirt path with steps/bridges	**Purple**: Whispering Cave (Purple Blazes on Trees) **Blue**: Buckeye Trail (Blue Blazes on Trees)
Distance:	**Access:**	**Wheelchair Access:**
5.0 miles. 2-3 hour hike Heavy Use. Plan a weekday trip. Hike early morning.	*Open dawn to dusk/365 days a year. *Well-behaved dogs on leash allowed.	No
Restrooms:	**Features:**	**Parking GPS:**
Yes, Visitor Center	Cliffs, Waterfalls, Rock Formations	39.436394, -82.539169

There are two places you can hop on the trail.
Trails are a one-way system.

1) You can start at the Visitor Center-There are steps at the Visitor Center near the kiosk.

2) You can also start at Upper Falls near that kiosk (as shown in images and on trail map).

Follow the blue trail markers (Buckeye Trail) down into the gorge and signs 1.5 miles to the Whispering Cave Purple Trail (it is marked with a sign). It will loop around one-way to Whispering Cave and back to the Visitor Center or Upper Falls.

Purple is the Old Man's Cave to Whispering Cave Trail Loop Trail (Purple Blazes on Trees)

Blue: Grandma Gatewood Trail and Buckeye Trail (Blue Blazes on Trees)

Interesting sights include: Cave and waterfall.

Whispering Cave Trail Map

Whispering Cave
Trail Map from
Lower Falls/Gorge:

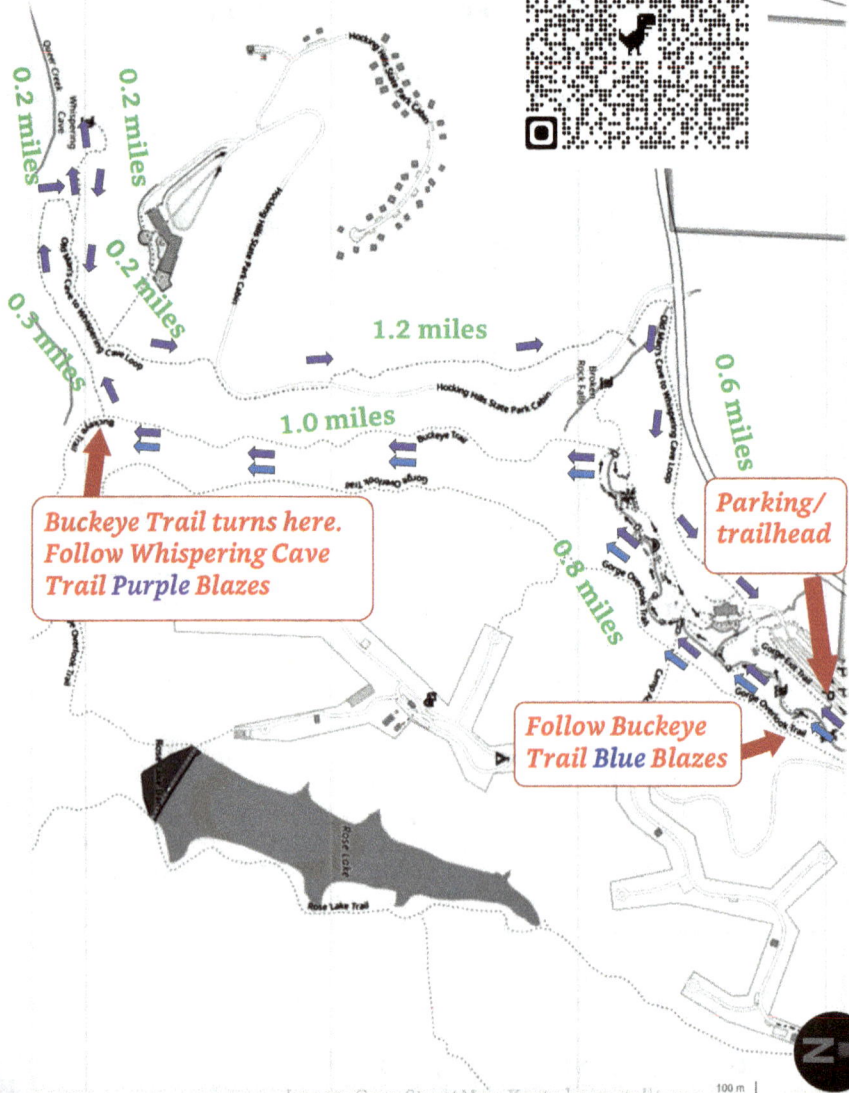

0.2 miles

0.2 miles

0.2 miles

0.2 miles

0.3 miles

1.2 miles

1.0 miles

0.6 miles

0.8 miles

Buckeye Trail turns here. Follow Whispering Cave Trail Purple Blazes

Parking/ trailhead

Follow Buckeye Trail Blue Blazes

Rose Lake

Rose Lake Trail

100 m
500 ft

Image: OpenStreetMap Karte hergestellt aus

Entrance at Old Man's Cave Parking Lot

Along Trail

Swinging Bridge

Whispering Cave

Hocking Hills State Park
Cantwell Cliffs

Cantwell Cliffs is one of the major hiking trails of Hocking Hills State Park. It was named for the family of Josiah and Joseph Cantwell, early settlers in the area. More remote, Cantwell Cliffs has sheer rock faces and a rock shelter. It offers two trails—one along the rim and the other through the gorge. A unique feature is "The Squeeze," a narrow passage along the trail.

Parking/Trailhead:

**Hocking Hills State Park
Cantwell Cliffs Parking/Trailhead
OH-374, Rockbridge, Ohio 43149
(39.540048, -82.575761)**

Hike: One-way Gorge Trail and One-way
Rim Trail, both starting at the parking lot. The trail is
strenuous with many steps. Most remote area. Hikers
must stay on the trail.

Type of Trail:	Quality:	Markings:
Loop	*Nature Trail *Dirt path with steps/bridges	**Yellow**: Bottom of Gorge (Yellow Blazes on Trees) **Red**: Top of the Gorge Rim Trail (Red Blazes)
Distance:	**Access:**	**Wheelchair Access:**
1.0 to 1.5 miles. 1-2 hour hike. Heavy Use. Plan a weekday trip. Hike early morning.	*Open dawn to dusk/365 days a year. *Well-behaved dogs on leash allowed. Cliffs.	No
Restrooms:	**Features:**	**Parking GPS:**
Yes, at Parking area	Cliffs, Waterfalls, Rock Formations	39.540048, -82.575761

There is a Rim Trail and a Gorge Trail:

Cantwell Gorge Trail: Hikers follow the Yellow Blazes to the Red Blazes for a total of 1.0 miles, including the parking lot.

Cantwell Rim Trail: Hikers follow the Red Blazes from the parking lot at the base of the cliff back along the rim and to the parking lot. About 1.5 miles.

Interesting sights include: Both can access The Squeeze at the start. Unique rock staircase.

Cantwell Cliffs Trail Map

Cantwell Cliffs Gorge/Rim Trail Map:

Gorge Trail blazed in Yellow

The Squeeze aka Fat Woman's Squeeze

Rim Trail blazed in Red

0.1 miles

0.2 miles

0.3 miles

0.4 miles

0.2 miles

Cantwell Rim Trail

Cantwell Gorge Trail

Cantwell Rim Trail

Cantwell Rim Trail

Hocking Hills Sta

Fat Woman's Squeeze

Cantwell Cliffs

Restrooms

P

N

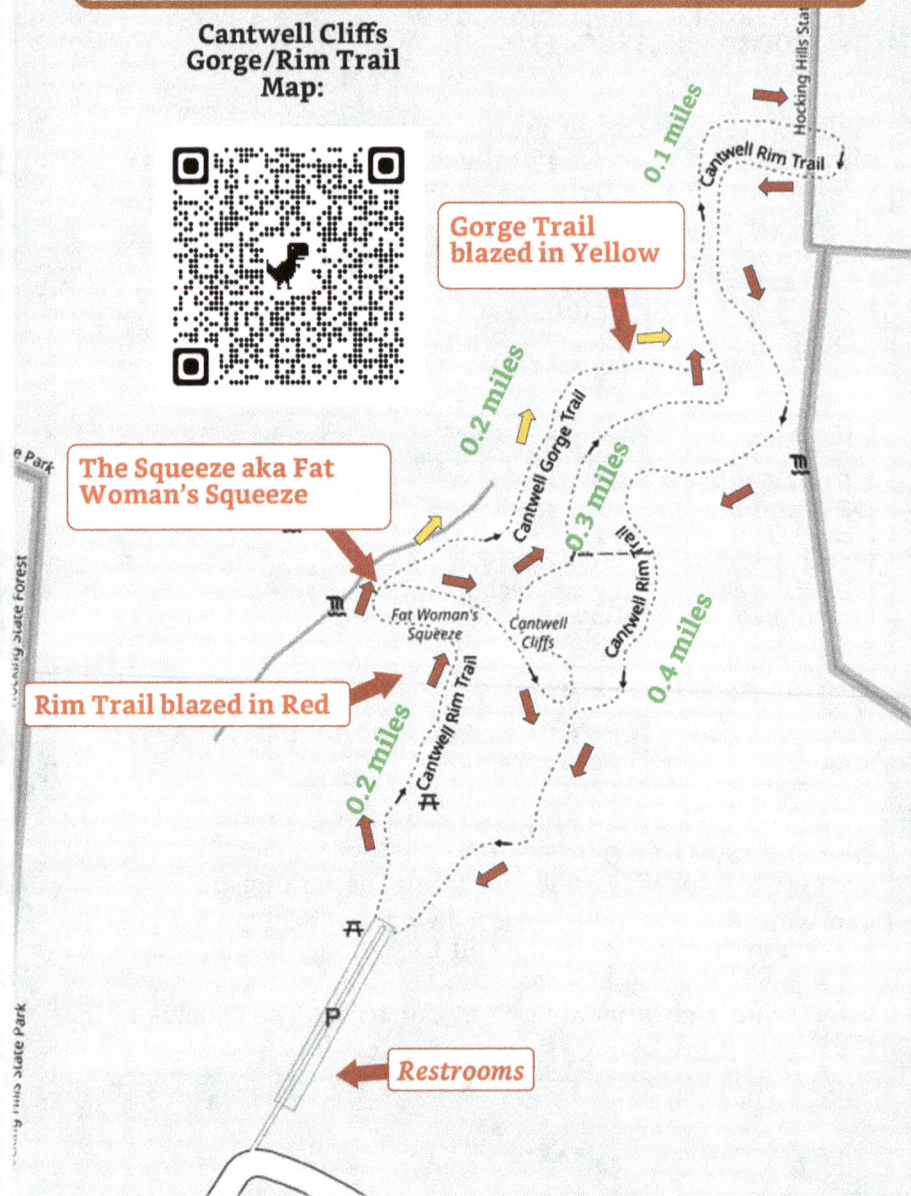

Image: OpenStreetMap

100 m
500 ft

Rim Trail blazed in red

Cantwell Cliffs

The Squeeze

Hocking Hills State Park
Rock House

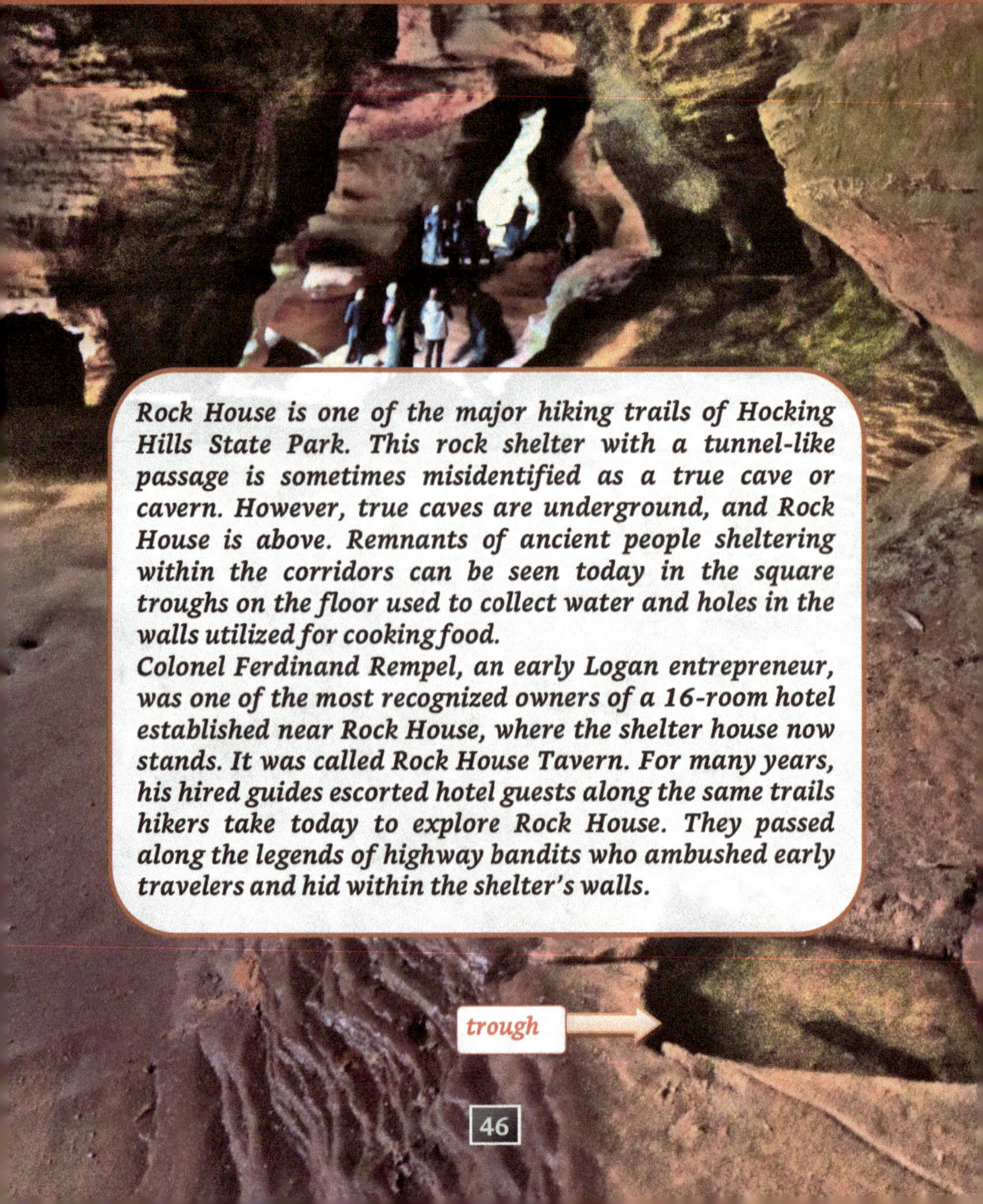

Rock House is one of the major hiking trails of Hocking Hills State Park. This rock shelter with a tunnel-like passage is sometimes misidentified as a true cave or cavern. However, true caves are underground, and Rock House is above. Remnants of ancient people sheltering within the corridors can be seen today in the square troughs on the floor used to collect water and holes in the walls utilized for cooking food.

Colonel Ferdinand Rempel, an early Logan entrepreneur, was one of the most recognized owners of a 16-room hotel established near Rock House, where the shelter house now stands. It was called Rock House Tavern. For many years, his hired guides escorted hotel guests along the same trails hikers take today to explore Rock House. They passed along the legends of highway bandits who ambushed early travelers and hid within the shelter's walls.

trough →

Parking/Trailhead:

Hocking Hills State Park
Rock House Parking/Trailhead
16350 OH-374
Laurelville, Ohio 43135
(39.496462, -82.615015)

Hike: There are two one-way loop trails —a Rim Trail and a Gorge Trail, approximately 1.0 miles each, starting and ending at the parking lots. Hikers must stay on trail.

Type of Trail:	Quality:	Markings:
Loop	*Nature Trail *Dirt path with steps/bridges	Yellow: Bottom of Gorge (Yellow Blazes on Trees) Red: Top of the Gorge Rim Trail (Red Blazes)
Distance:	**Access:**	**Wheelchair Access:**
1.0 miles Heavy Use. Plan a weekday trip. Hike early morning.	*Open dawn to dusk/365 days a year. *Well-behaved dogs on leash allowed. Cliffs.	No
Restrooms:	**Features:**	**Parking GPS:**
Yes, Parking lot	Cliffs, Recess cave, Rock Formations	39.496462, -82.615015

There is a Rim Trail and a Gorge Trail:

Rock House Loop Trail is about 1.0 miles. Hikers enter from either the upper or lower parking lot, but both trails come together and exit at the shelter house/parking lot (at the top). The trail is rugged with steps and bridges. The tunnel-like shelter is about 25 feet high and 200 feet long.

Interesting sights include: Ancient people's cooking holes in the rock wall and water troughs on the floor. Shelter House at the top was the location of an old hotel.

Rock House Trail Map

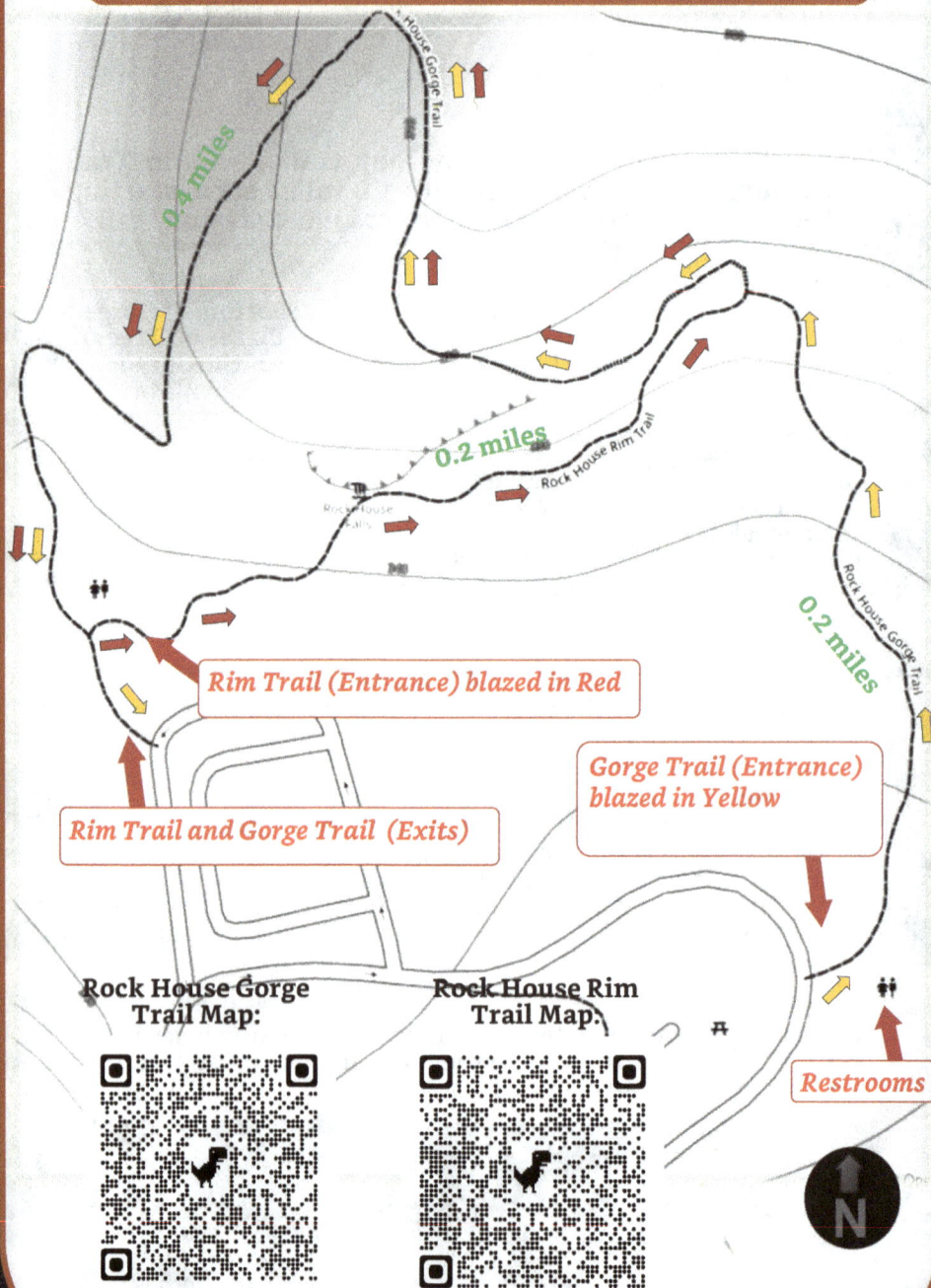

0.4 miles

Rock House Gorge Trail

0.2 miles

Rock House Rim Trail

Rock House Stairs

0.2 miles

Rock House Gorge Trail

Rim Trail (Entrance) blazed in Red

Gorge Trail (Entrance) blazed in Yellow

Rim Trail and Gorge Trail (Exits)

Rock House Gorge Trail Map:

Rock House Rim Trail Map:

Restrooms

N

100 m
500 ft

Image: OpenStreetMap

Trail in Winter

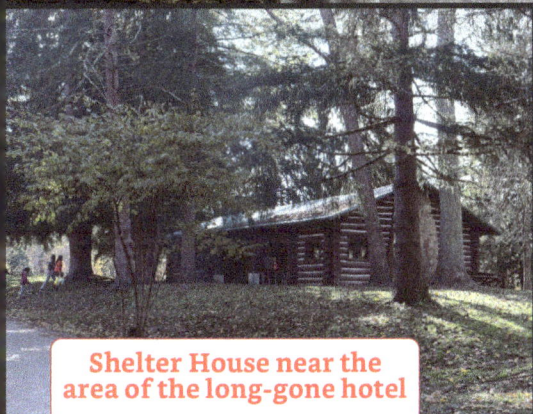

Shelter House near the area of the long-gone hotel

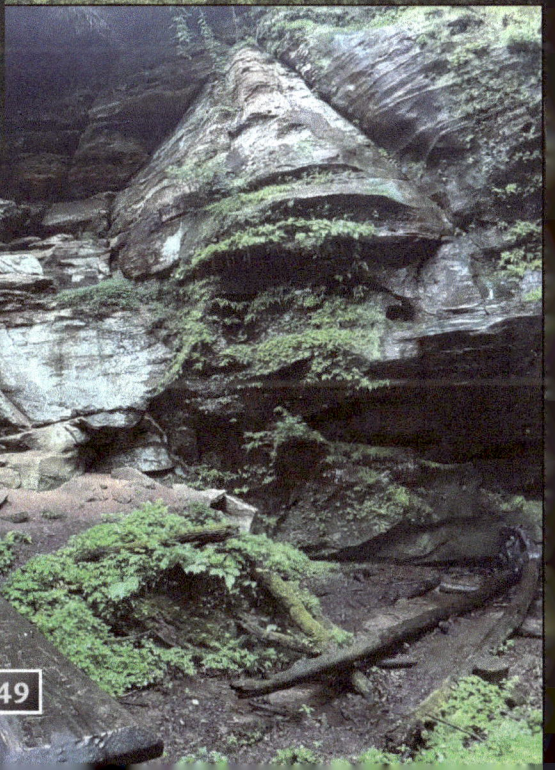

Hocking State Forest
Honor Camp Trail

In the 1950s, the Ohio State Penitentiary established several Honor Camps as work camps for prisoners around state parks and forests. One was in the Hocking Hills and is where the Hocking State Forestry buildings are today. The camps housed 20 to 60 inmates working with forestry divisions and state parks—clearing brush, planting trees, maintaining roadways, and even fighting forest fires. The men who worked here were given more opportunities than those in the prisons—not only were there no fence enclosures, they could dress in blue jeans and shirts, sign out for a couple of hours, and hike Conkle's Hollow. They even had a softball team.

The Division of Forestry Honor Camp Trail blends the history and beauty of the Hocking Hills with information on the challenges and opportunities available due to the influence of climate change on the natural environment specific to the region. Ten interpretive trail signs along the path highlight how climate change impacts local forest species and best management practices.

Parking/Trailhead:

Hocking State Forest
Honor Camp Trail Parking
State Route 374
Logan, Ohio 43138
(39.458783, -82.581029)

Hike: The loop trail is approximately 1.6 miles long and begins at an old service road near the gravel parking area.

Type of Trail:	Quality:	Markings:
Loop with a spur to waterfall	*Nature Trail *Dirt path	White Honor Camp Trail Purple for Spur Trail
Distance:	**Access:**	**Wheelchair Access:**
1.6 miles Takes 1-2 hours to hike.	*Open dawn to dusk/365 days a year.	No
Restrooms:	**Features:**	**Parking GPS:**
No	Cliffs, Waterfalls	39.458783, -82.581029

A small gravel parking area is 0.3 miles past the Division of Forestry offices. Hikers begin at a graveled access roadway just after the parking area with an orange forestry gate, following it upward and continuing on the same road (also a Right of Way) until it veers to the left. (The Right of Way continues onward). Stay on the grassy road/trail, and soon you will begin seeing the trail signs marked with: *Honor Camp Trail.*

The wide trail roams in and out of the forest (marked with the Honor Camp Trail signs or white pole signs with a Forestry emblem) and eventually fades into a dirt trail and beautiful stands of hemlocks. The trail veers to the left just as you see yellow-orange blazes on the trees, avoiding the private property. It continues downward, and it is here that hikers **will note the purple trail signs for the spur to the waterfall and caves.**

The Purple Trail Out: After, continue to follow the white and purple trail signs. There will be a fork where the purple signs will lead hikers upward, across a Right of Way, then across the Hocking State Forest Horse Trail. Hikers who continue on the Purple Trail will end up at the backside of the Forestry Offices. It is suggested to follow (at the point of the horse trail) the white signs back past the pond and to the gravel parking lot.

The Honor Camp White Trail out: Continue on the White Trail, and it crosses the Right of Way. When hikers get to the Right of Way, the opposite side of the trail is just a bit left of the direct trail. Watch for a very small stack of rocks used to mark the path. This trail is between the Right of Way and a gorge edge, following above another stunning gorge area. The direct pathway is difficult to see with thick leaves, but if you cannot find it, follow the gorge's rim at a safe distance. This trail will lead past the pond to the gravel parking area.

Honor Camp Trail

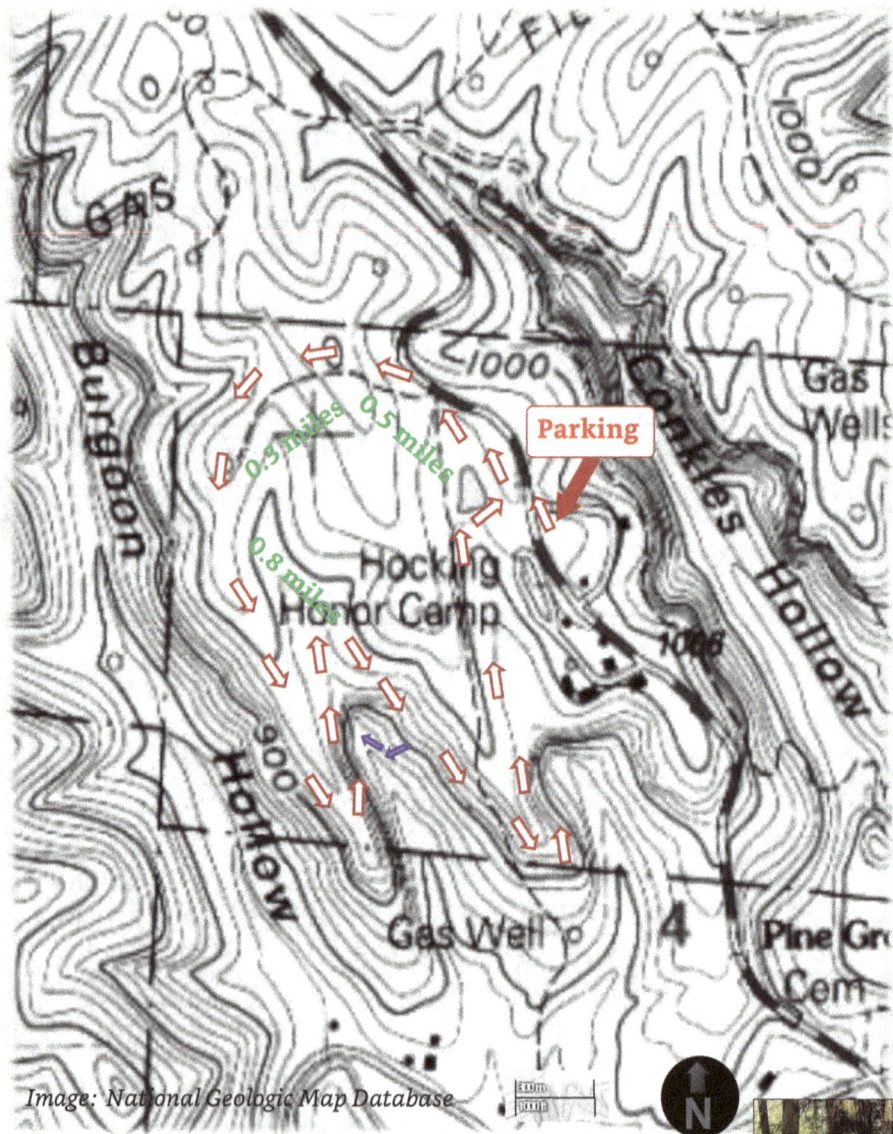

Image: National Geologic Map Database

You may see blue markings on the base of some trees. Do not follow these as blazes; they are marking trees chemically treated for wooly adelgid, an invasive, aphid-like insect attacking the hemlocks.

First veer in trail

Parking

Trailhead

Interpretive signs

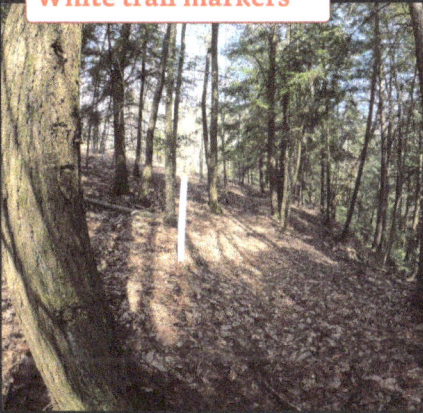

White trail markers

Purple spur marker

Waterfall

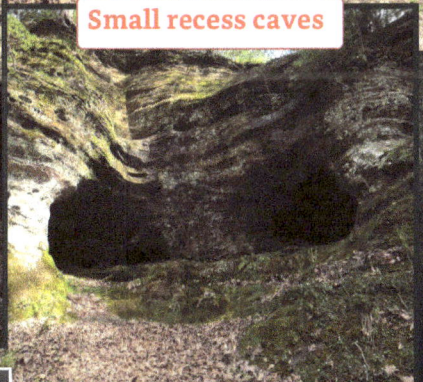

Small recess caves

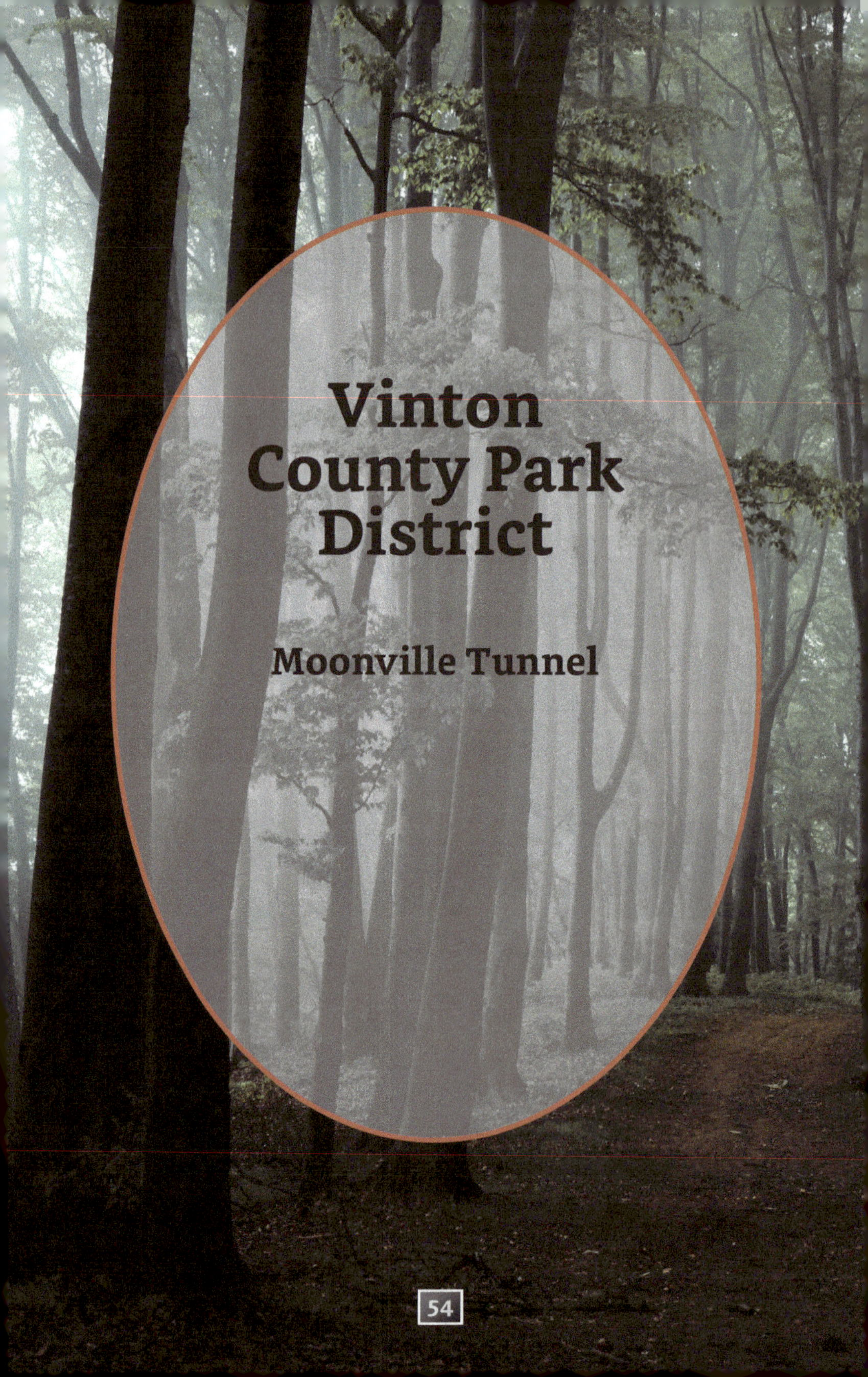

Vinton County Park District

Moonville Tunnel

Moonville Rail Trail

Image: OpenStreetMap

Vinton County Parks
Moonville Tunnel

There was once a small mining community along the Marietta and Cincinnati railroad tracks called Moonville, taking its name from the breathtaking way Earth's only natural satellite showed itself above the tunnel in the dark of night. Although only a couple of families lived in the town proper, people from Zaleski, Hope Furnace Station, Ingham Station, and even Athens used the straight path of the tracks cutting through the steep hills to travel to neighboring towns. It was much better than following the roadway, which went up and down steep hills and often flooded as it followed Raccoon Creek. Unfortunately, the number of people using the tracks and the fast trains barreling along its path made for many deaths. Numerous legends have arisen that the ghosts of some of the dead return, including an engineer killed when two trains collided in November of 1880 and a town bully who tosses stones from above the tunnel at those walking beneath.

Parking/Trailhead:

Vinton County Park District
Moonville Tunnel Parking/Trailhead
Hope-Moonville Road
Zaleski, Ohio 45698
(39.308368, -82.324567)

Hike: Hikers can follow the out and back, level rail-trail to Moonville Tunnel and then to King Tunnel. In the spring, summer, and autumn, bring mosquito repellent!

Type of Trail:	Quality:	Markings:
Out and Back	*Rail-trail *Level *Multi-use (gravel) Hiker/Biker/Horses	None. Rail-trail path is easy to follow
Distance:	**Access:**	**Wheelchair Access:**
-0.2 miles (to Moonville Tunnel) 2 minutes -2.8 miles (to King Tunnel) One-way - 3.0 hours out and back	*Open dawn to dusk/365 days a year. *Well-behaved dogs on leash allowed.	No, only if wheelchair can use packed pebbled gravel with a mild step up at the bridge over Raccoon Creek.
Restrooms:	**Features:**	**Parking GPS:**
No	Tunnels, waterways, bridges, ghost town	39.308368, -82.324567

From Moonville to Kings Tunnel:

Hikers can follow the rail-trail from Moonville and across the bridge over Raccoon Creek 0.2 miles to Moonville Tunnel.

For a longer walk, hikers can continue another 2.7 miles one-way along the rail-trail and across a series of bridges (once train trestles) to King Tunnel. Total hike 5.8 miles. About 2 to 3 hours.

Interesting sights include: The brick Moonville Tunnel and the wooden King Tunnel.
Along the way, hikers will pass Bear Hollow which is home to many beavers and their dams.
Before crossing the road to King Tunnel, watch for a long fence on the right. This area was once the town of Kings Station, a mining community.
Just after King Tunnel, look across the pond on the left. You will see a large boulder that was made into a root cellar. At one time, it even housed the pigs of a local landowner!

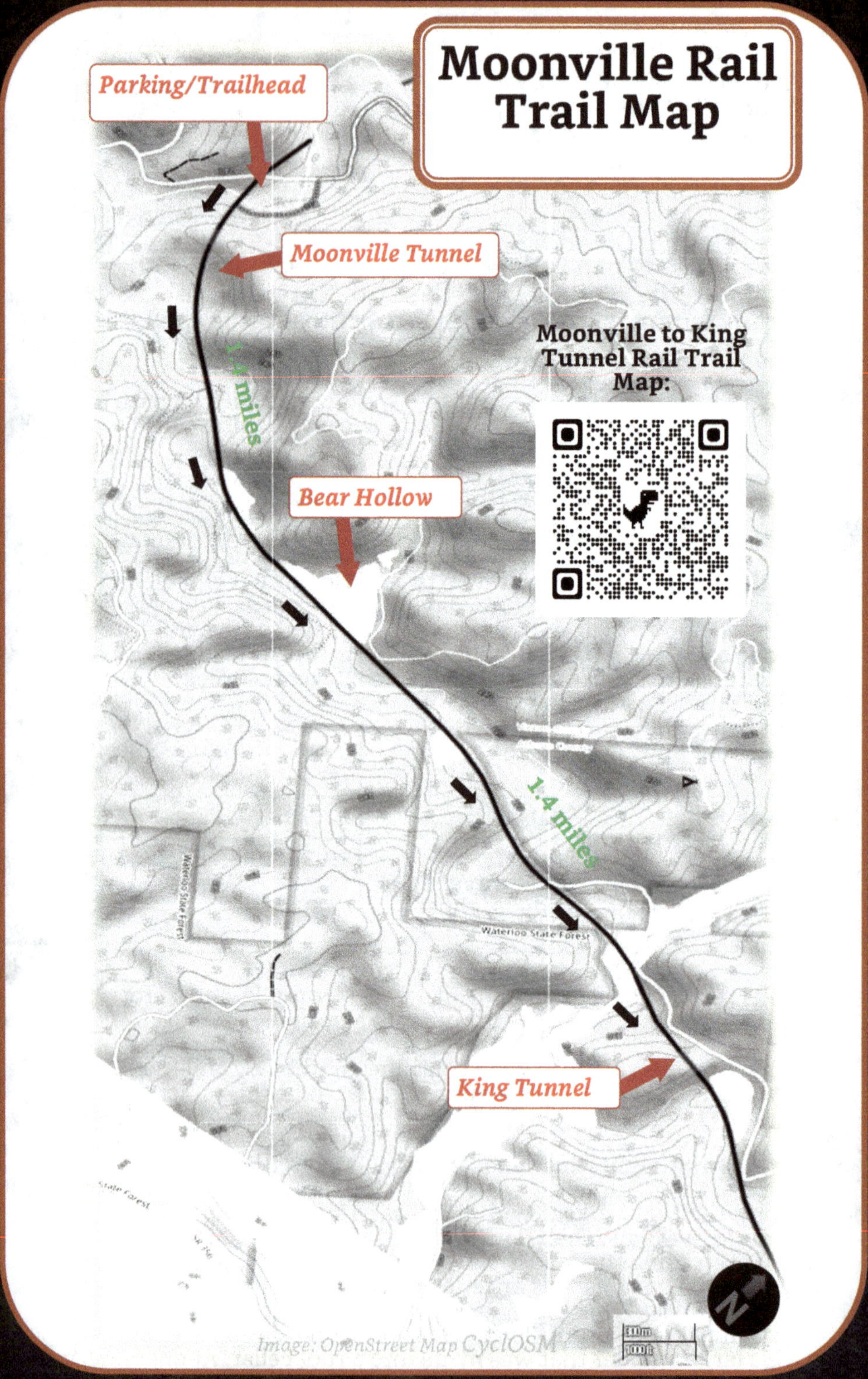

Moonville Rail Trail Map

Parking/Trailhead

Moonville Tunnel

1.4 miles

Bear Hollow

Moonville to King Tunnel Rail Trail Map:

1.4 miles

Waterloo State Forest

King Tunnel

Image: OpenStreet Map CyclOSM

Moonville Tunnel

Bear Hollow

King Tunnel

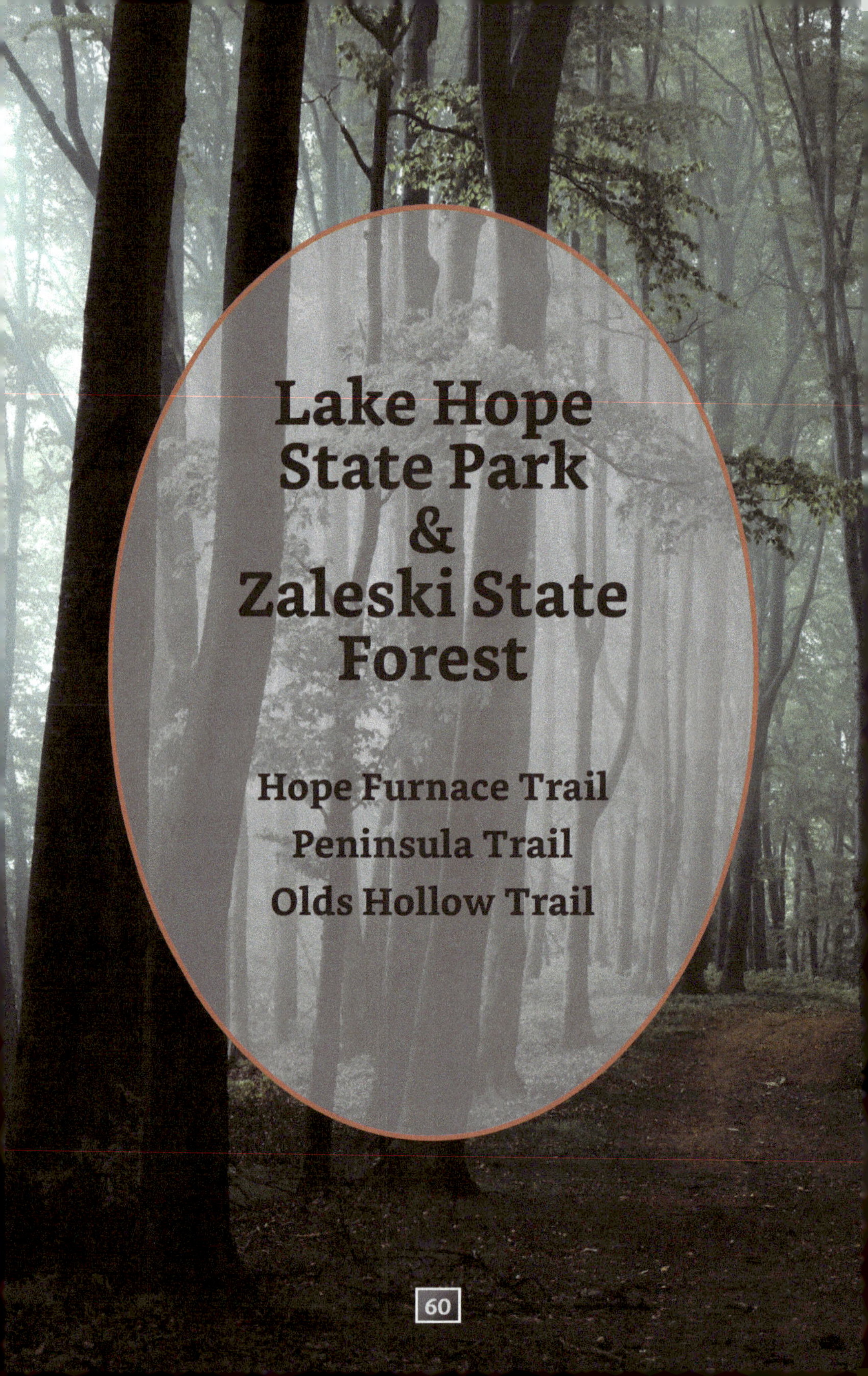

Lake Hope State Park & Zaleski State Forest

Hope Furnace Trail
Peninsula Trail
Olds Hollow Trail

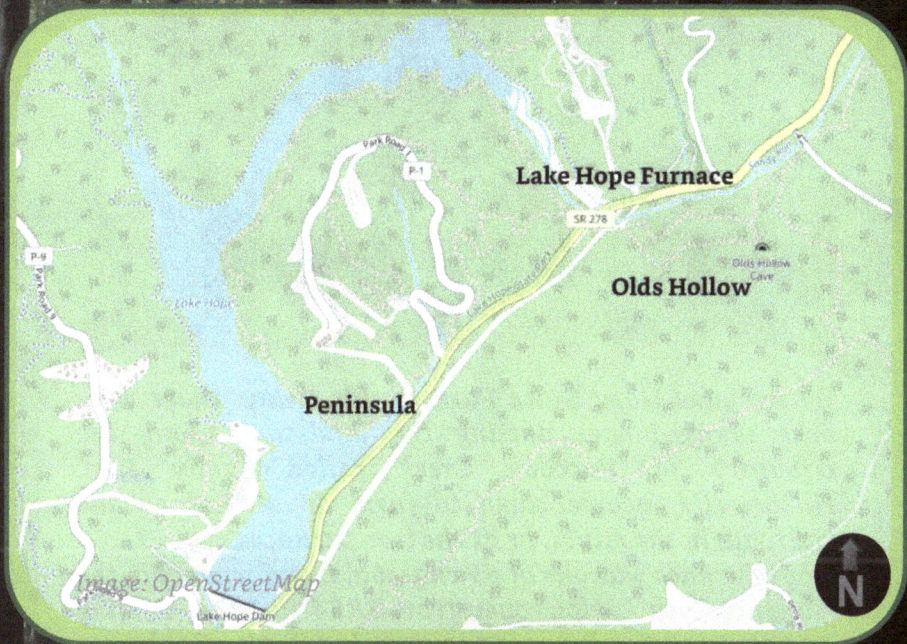

Lake Hope Furnace

Olds Hollow

Peninsula

Image: OpenStreetMap

Lake Hope State Park

Hope Furnace Trail

Where Lake Hope State Park stands today, there were once many homes dotting the landscape along the tributary of Raccoon Creek called Sandy Run. Historically, people came to farm or worked on the railroad, in the mines, or at the iron furnaces.

Hope Furnace was one of 69 charcoal iron furnaces in the Hanging Rock Region, open from 1854 to 1874. Fueling and running the furnace required hundreds of laborers who worked there, cutting timber or driving oxen teams to haul the ore. The charcoal (made by stacking, then burning cut wood) used to fuel the furnace was produced in the surrounding forest, then transported by oxen. From a nearby town called Hope Furnace Station, a horse would pull a railcar along a spur and up to the furnace, where laborers loaded the finished product, iron. Then the railcar would return to the station. Many workers and families lived across the road from the furnace in cabins. Little remains of the town's past except for the ruins of Hope Furnace. Only foundation stones from the homes endure across the roadway where a pine grove now stands.

Parking/Trailhead:
Lake Hope State Park
Lake Hope Beach Road
McArthur, Ohio 45651
(39.324943, -82.355022)

Hike: Out and back trail along the shoreline of Lake Hope to Hope Furnace ruins.

Type of Trail:	Quality:	Markings:
Out and Back	*Developed Trail *Dirt path with bridges	No blazes
Distance:	**Access:**	**Wheelchair Access:**
2.9 miles, one way. Total 5.7 miles.	*Open dawn to dusk/365 days a year. *Well-behaved dogs on leash allowed.	No
Restrooms:	**Features:**	**Parking GPS:**
Yes, at historical furnace ruins	Rock Formations, forest, lake	39.324943, -82.355022

Hikers follow a rugged dirt trail along the shoreline of Lake Hope and to the ruins of the Hope Furnace. There are a few signs showing the trail map, but no blazes.

Interesting sights include: In spring, watch for daffodils blooming near the trail which, many times, shows where old homesteads were located as some who farmed the land planted these flowers around the home and they still bloom today.

There is a local legend that a worker at Hope Furnace fell into the fiery stack one night on his shift. Afterward, those working in the nearby buildings would hear mysterious knocks on the doors. When those within opened the door, nobody was there. Some have even seen a ghostly lantern bobbing up and down above the furnace. It is believed to be the ghost of the worker who met his doom there.

Eagles make their home here seasonally and they can be seen flying over the lake, oftentimes in the coves.
Hikers can also make a side hike by crossing State Route 278 and hopping on the Olds Hollow Trail at (39.330900, -82.341080). The trail starts after a short walk across the bridge over Sandy Run along State Route 278.

Hope Furnace Trail Map

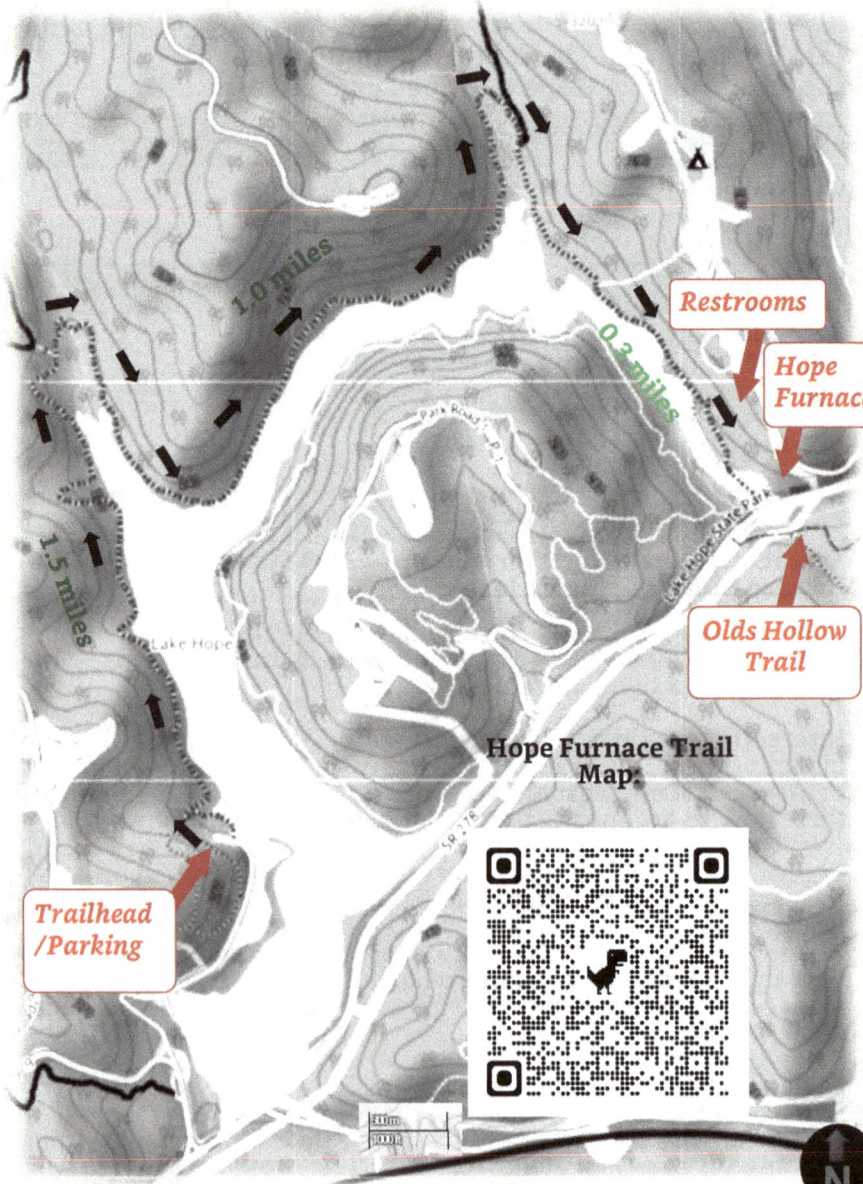

1.0 miles

0.2 miles

1.5 miles

Restrooms

Hope Furnace

Olds Hollow Trail

Trailhead /Parking

Hope Furnace Trail Map:

Image: OpenStreet CyclOSM

N

Trailhead

Along the trail

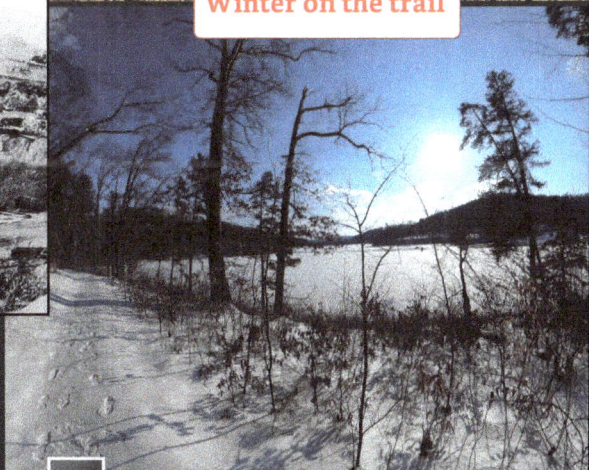
Hope Furnace in its heyday

Winter on the trail

Lake Hope State Park

Peninsula Trail

The Peninsula Trail at Lake Hope State Park parallels the lake's shoreline much of the way. It is a rugged path with beautiful views of the water. It has many wildflowers along the trail during the spring and early summer, including Spring Beauty, Common Violet, Cutleaf Toothwort, Large-Flowered Trillium, Rue Anemone, Fire Pink, Bloodroot, and Wild Geranium. Hikers may see Bald Eagles taking flight and riding the wind here and occasionally hear the huffing snort of a startled white-tailed deer.

Parking/Trailhead:
Lake Hope State Park
Pull-off along State Route 278
McArthur, Ohio 45651
(39.327041, -82.346750)

Hike: The loop trail is approximately 3.1 miles long and begins near a gravel pull-off at the entrance to Lodge Road.

Type of Trail:	Quality:	Markings:
Loop	*Developed Trail *Dirt path with steps/bridges	No
Distance:	**Access:**	**Wheelchair Access:**
3.1 miles Takes about 1.5 to 2 hours to hike.	*Open dawn to dusk/365 days a year. *Well-behaved dogs on leash allowed.	No
Restrooms:	**Features:**	**Parking GPS:**
Yes, by taking a short hike off the main Peninsula Trail along State Route 278 where Hope Furnace comes into view. Pit latrines are available at Hope Furnace.	**Forest, Lake, Historical iron furnace**	39.327041, -82.346750

Peninsula Trail is a loop trail. Hikers start at the trail sign on the same side of Lodge Road as the small gravel pull-off on State Route 278 and end just across Lodge Road.

Hikers follow a rugged dirt trail along the shoreline and coves of Lake Hope. Along the way, Hope Furnace comes into view across Sandy Run before hikers turn and slowly work upwards in elevation to the top of a hill. A few signs show the trail map and the hiker's location. There are no trail blazes.

Hikers can also make a side hike near the point where the Peninsula Trail and Greenbrier Trail intersect for a short period by crossing State Route 278 and hopping on the Olds Hollow Trail at (39.330900, -82.341080). It is near Hope Furnace.

Interesting sights include: Watch for Bald Eagles in the coves.

Peninsula Trail Map

Peninsula Trail Map:

Restrooms

Hope Furnace

1.3 miles

0.2 miles

Olds Hollow Trail

1.0 miles

0.6 miles

Trailhead /Parking

Lake Hope

N

Image: OpenStreet Map CyclOSM

100 m
500 ft

Along the trail

Trailhead

Lake Hope State Park
Olds Hollow

Mary Olds had property across from Hope Furnace, and the valley there was named Olds Hollow.

The land between State Route 278 and the pine forest along the Olds Hollow Trail had small wooden homes for the furnace workers. Little remains to show a town thrived here as the land was deforested during the early to mid-1800s. Later, CCC workers planted the pines that are still there today. A cemetery was established on the side of a tall hill around 1853 and called Pioneer Cemetery. Families buried fifty to sixty who died in and around the community here, although few stones remain.

Parking/Trailhead:

Lake Hope State Park/Zaleski State Forest
State Route 278 McArthur, Ohio 45651
Parking: (39.331584, -82.339796)
Trailhead:(39.330889, -82.341083)

Hike: Loop trail is 1.5 miles long. Begins near a Zaleski Backpack Trail parking lot, but is also accessible by the Peninsula Trail and Hope Furnace Trail.

Type of Trail:	Quality:	Markings:
Loop	*Developed Trail *Dirt path with steps/bridges	Blue: (Blue Blazes on Trees) Overlaps with orange Backpack Trail
Distance:	**Access:**	**Wheelchair Access:**
1.5 miles Takes about an hour to hike. May be muddy.	*Open dawn to dusk/365 days a year. *Well-behaved dogs on leash allowed.	No
Restrooms:	**Features:**	**Parking GPS:**
At Hope Furnace	Forest, Cave	39.331584, -82.339796

Hikers can take this trail (via a loop formed by Olds Hollow Trail marked in blue and X-Y sections of the Zaleski Backpack Trail marked in orange) off Peninsula Trail, Hope Furnace Trail, or by parking at the Zaleski Backpack Trail and Hope Furnace lots. To get to the trailhead, hikers must walk southwest along the berm of State Route 278 (over the bridge on the road crossing Sandy Run). After, it crosses a small stream and heads upward into a thick pine forest once a part of the community of Hope Furnace. There is a puddle at the beginning of the trail sign; remnants of an old spring once used by the town still wets the path.

Looking closely, those passing through the forest may see traces of old homes and buildings buried beneath years of pine needles. Hikers can take a spur trail to a small recess cave not far along the path and near a wooden bridge. After, the trail meanders through the woods, along a creek valley, and another recess cave. Between, Pioneer Cemetery is located on top of one hill. Few headstones remain, but this was once a main graveyard for early settlers and those who lived near the iron furnace.

As the trail loops to the end, look across the wetland and creek and past State Route 278. Before Hope Furnace, you will see a road where Hope Furnace Schoolhouse was once the teaching hub for the community, although the building was demolished years ago.

Interesting sights include: Just before crossing the first bridge, hikers will see a spur trail leading to a small recess cave. A second recess cave is located on the right before hikers begin the X-Y section of the Backpack Trail for the final jog of the Olds Hollow Loop Trail.

Olds Hollow Trail Map

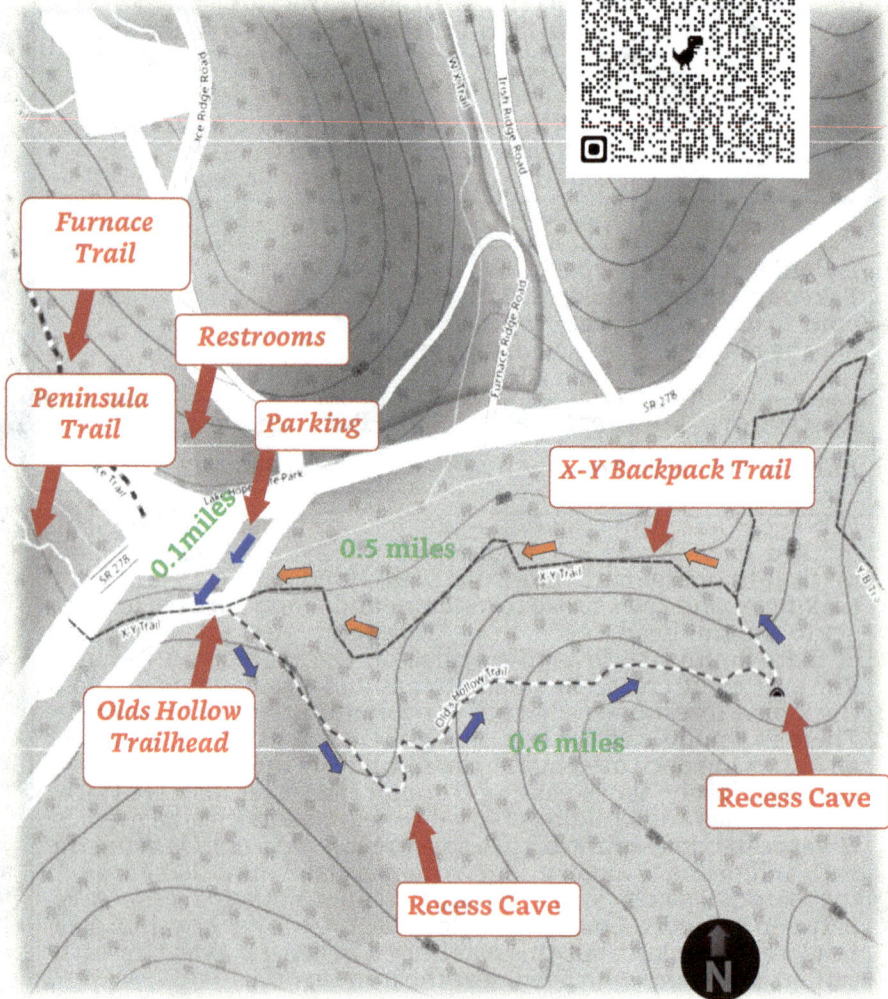

Olds Hollow Trail Map:

Furnace Trail

Restrooms

Peninsula Trail

Parking

0.1 miles

0.5 miles

X-Y Backpack Trail

Olds Hollow Trailhead

0.6 miles

Recess Cave

Recess Cave

Image: OpenStreet style CyclOSM

Trailhead

Loop Trail Start/End

Orange blazes

Recess Cave

Pioneer Cemetery

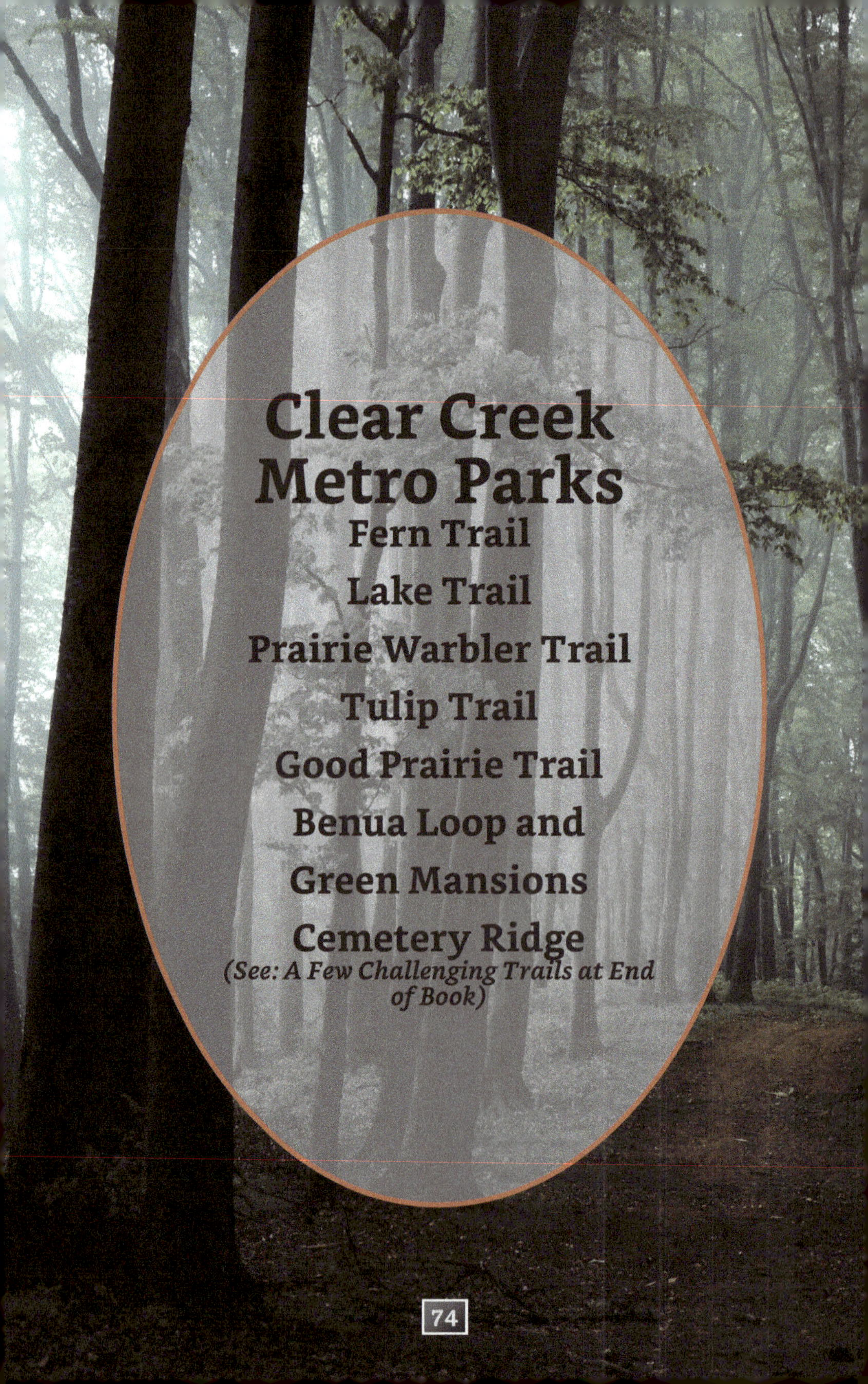

Clear Creek
Metro Parks

Fern Trail

Lake Trail

Prairie Warbler Trail

Tulip Trail

Good Prairie Trail

Benua Loop and

Green Mansions

Cemetery Ridge

(See: A Few Challenging Trails at End of Book)

Lake/Tulip/Prairie/Fern

Cemetery Ridge Trail
See "A Few Challenging Trails"

Benua/Green Mansions

Clear Creek
Metro Park

Clear Creek Road

Clear Creek Road

Buena Vista Road

CR 34

Image: OpenStreetMap

N

Clear Creek Metro Park
Fern Trail

In the late 1960s and early 1970s, the Army Corps of Engineers proposed building a flood control impoundment at the confluence of Clear Creek and the Hocking River. The dam would flood major sections of the Clear Creek Valley, home to many families and areas that embraced the unique and rare character of the Hocking Hills region. However, with the help of public opposition and several families who owned property there and donated their lands for preservation (the Benuas, Becks, and Barnebeys), the government refused to fund the project. Eventually, the land became Clear Creek Metro Park with its many diverse trails—including Fern Trail, offering everything that makes the park distinctive. Hikers will pass old oak and maple forests to patches of sweet-smelling hemlocks and even trek along meadows, streams, and sandstone outcroppings.

Parking/Trailhead:
Clear Creek Metro Park
Fern Picnic Area Parking
Clear Creek Road
Rockbridge, Ohio 43149
(39.588502, -82.59435)

Hike: Fern Creek Loop Trail is about 1.9 miles long and begins as a spur across Clear Creek Road from Fern Picnic Area. It is mildly strenuous. Hikers must stay on trail.

Type of Trail:	Quality:	Markings:
Loop (starts off as a spur)	*Developed Trail *Dirt path with steep ridge	No Blazes Occasional maps along trail. *Be advised: Trail color markings on maps are similar and faded and are difficult to distinguish.*

Distance:	Access:	Wheelchair Access:
1.9 miles Takes about 1 to 1.5 hours to hike.	*Open dawn to dusk/365 days a year. *No Dogs Allowed	No

Restrooms:	Features:	Parking GPS:
No	Meadows, Forest, Creeks	39.588502, -82.59435

Hikers park at Fern Picnic Area and walk across Clear Creek Road to a spur trail that leads 0.2 miles to the Fern Trail loop. Hikers can choose left or right at the fork to begin the loop. When turning left, there is a gradual uphill climb through hemlocks and pines and even a grassy section of meadow. On the return, the hike is downhill near a gently-flowing creek and beneath many hemlocks.
Interesting sights include:

When entering the park, you will pass a local landmark, Leaning Rock, a unique rock formation welcoming visitors to Clear Creek.

Fern Trail Map

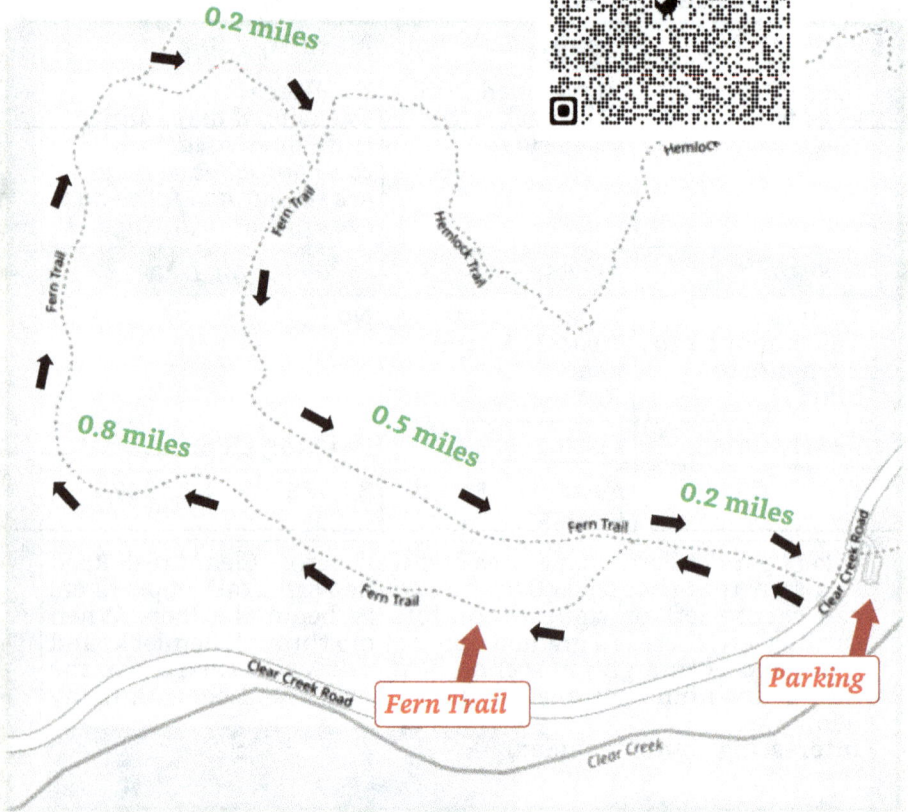

Fern Trail Map:

0.2 miles

Fern Trail

Hemlock Trail

Hemlock

0.8 miles

0.5 miles

0.2 miles

Fern Trail

Fern Trail

Fern Trail

Clear Creek Road

Clear Creek Road

Fern Trail

Parking

Clear Creek

Image: OpenStreet Map

N

100 m
500 ft

Trailhead spur

Fern Trail

Meadows

Maps Along Trail

Along Trail

Clear Creek Metro Park

Barnebey-Hambleton Day Use Area

Lake Trail. Prairie Warbler Trail.
Tulip Tree Trail. Good Prairie Trail

Four Short Trails

In the farther reaches of the park, visitors can explore four separate loop trails in the Barnebey-Hambleton Area. The Barnebey-Hambleton Area was once part of a Church Youth Camp called Camp Indianola, created by Oscar Barnebey in the 1920s. He built Lake Ramona by damming a tributary of Clear Creek and built cabins and a camp lodge nearby. The camp operated for over forty years, run by church organizations. Mister Barnebey eventually turned the property over in the 1970s to Ohio State University as an outdoor laboratory for field trips; then, in the 1990s, the land was purchased by the Metro Parks.

Parking/Trailhead:

Clear Creek Metro Park
Barnebey-Hambleton Day Use Area
Unnamed Road off Clear Creek Road SW
Lancaster, Ohio 43130

(39.600344, -82.631620)
(There is a sign along Clear Creek Road directing traffic to the Barnebey-Hambleton Day Use Area.)

Hike: **Four hiking trails in the Barnebey-Hambleton Day Use Area of the park. Hikers must stay on trail.**

Type of Trail:	Quality:	Markings:
Loops	*Nature Trail *Dirt path with steps/bridges	No
Distance:	**Access:**	**Wheelchair Access:**
Trails: *Lake : 1.2 miles *Prairie Warbler: 0.6 miles *Tulip Tree: 0.6 miles *Good Prairie: 0.3 miles	*Open dawn to dusk/365 days a year. *No Dogs Allowed	No
Restrooms:	**Features:**	**Parking GPS:**
Yes, near parking lot	Lake, Woodland	39.600344, -82.631620

Hikers can choose from 4 Trails:

Lake Trail: From the parking lot near Valley View Picnic Area, hikers cross the road to Lake Trail. The trail follows a dirt path through the woods and down to a spur to Lake Ramona and the observation deck.

Prairie Warbler Trail: Hikers trek a rolling hill among meadows and woods. Good Prairie Trail is accessed partially along this trail.

Tulip Trail: This trail loops through the woodland and along a hillside.

Good Prairie Trail: Short hike running around a prairie. To reach the trail, you must take Prairie Warbler Trail.

Interesting sights include: These hiking trails cover a multitude of habitats, from prairie to lake, offering easy, quick access to a wide variety of bird, mammal, and flower species.

Barnebey-Hambleton Day Use Area Trail Map

Clear Creek Tulip Trail:

Clear Creek Lake Trail:

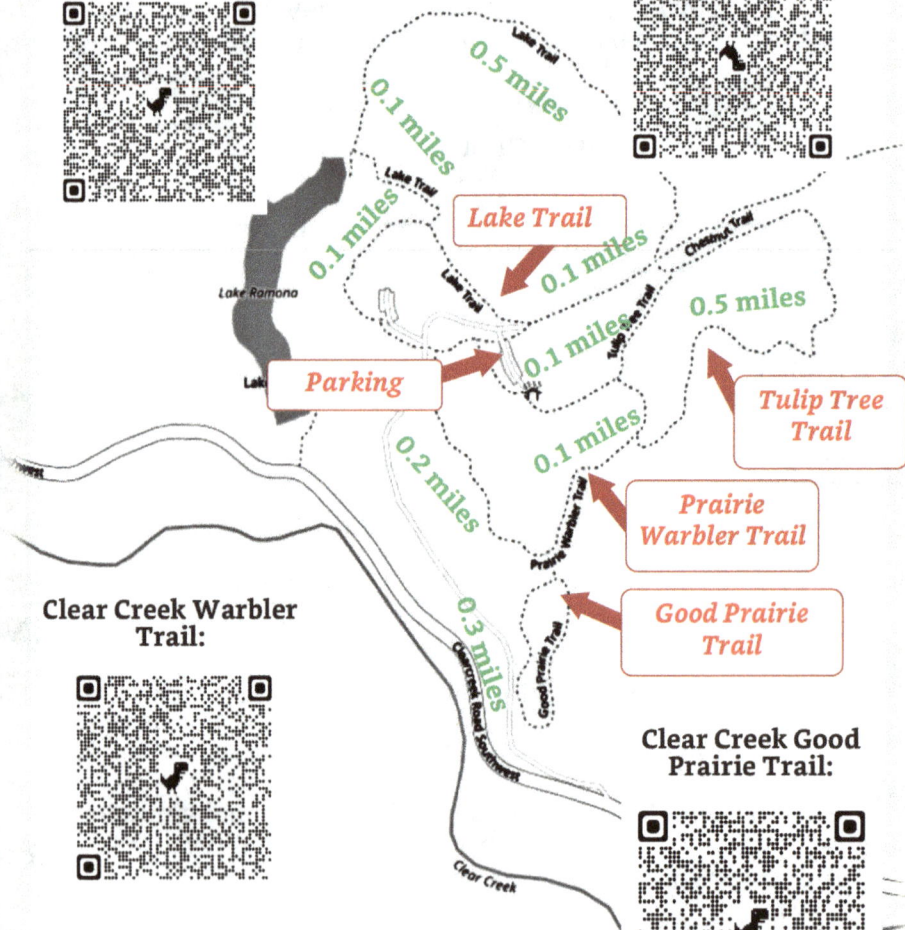

Lake Trail

0.5 miles

0.1 miles

0.1 miles

Lake Trail

Lake Trail

Chestnut Trail

Lake Trail

0.1 miles

0.1 miles

Lake Ramona

0.5 miles

Parking

0.1 miles

Tulip Tree Trail

0.2 miles

Prairie Warbler Trail

Prairie Warbler Trail

Good Prairie Trail

0.3 miles

Good Prairie Trail

Clear Creek Warbler Trail:

Charcoal Road Southwest

Clear Creek

Clear Creek Good Prairie Trail:

N

Image: OpenStreet Map

100 m
500 ft

Lake Trail

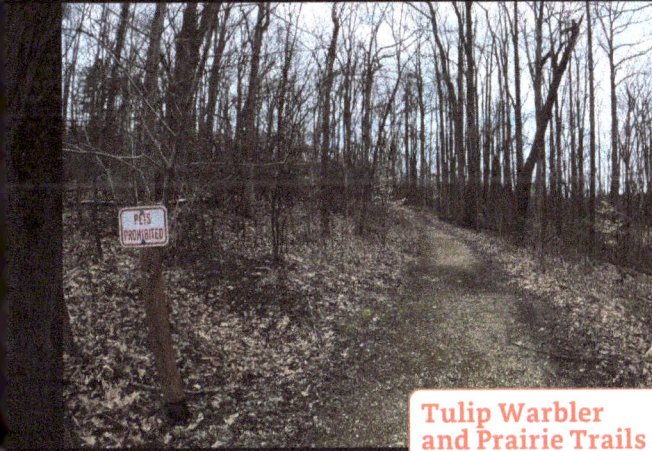

Tulip Warbler
and Prairie Trails

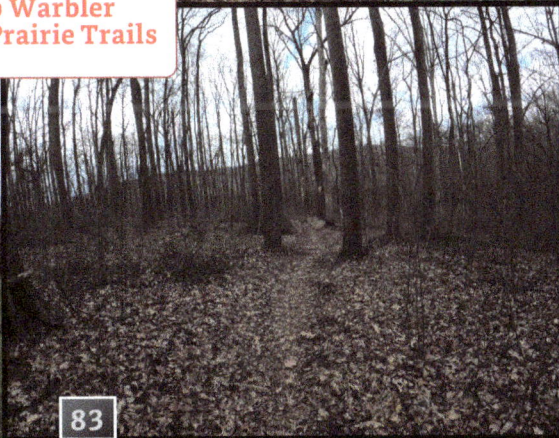

Clear Creek Metro Park

Benua Loop Trail
Green Mansions Spur

This loop goes through the property once owned by conservationists Emily and William Benua who were instrumental in stopping the destruction of the area by the Army Corps of Engineers when plans were made to build a dam on the Hocking River and Clear Creek, flooding the region. They later donated the property to The Nature Conservancy and it was transferred to Metro Parks. The trail follows along dirt paths and old, gravel township roads through the forest, then to the ruins of the family's mansion and a lake.

Parking/Trailhead:
Clear Creek Metro Park
Parking Area behind Park Office
Off Clear Creek Road
(39.592831, -82.623669)

Hike: This loop trail follows dirt paths
and old roads with a spur to the remnants of an old
mansion, then along a meadow. Great place for birding
offering different habitats. Hikers must stay on trail.

Type of Trail:	Quality:	Markings:
Loop Spur	*Nature Trail *Dirt path with steps/bridges *Trail Road	No
Distance:	**Access:**	**Wheelchair Access:**
Loop: 3.0 miles Spur: about 0.4 miles, one-way 1.5 to 3 hour hike.	*Open dawn to dusk/365 days a year. *No Dogs Allowed	No
Restrooms:	**Features:**	**Parking GPS:**
No	Forest, Abandoned mansion and buildings	39.592831, -82.623669 Road to lot is between white house (which is the park office) and a barn

Hikers can find the parking area by pulling into the drive
between the white office building and a barn and following the
roadway until it stops at a small gravel lot just before a concrete
bridge across Clear Creek.

The trail begins as a spur by crossing the concrete bridge and,
after, a grassy path. It then forks near an old homesite which is
the start and end point of the loop. Take a left (if you like the
strenuous uphill climb on the way in and an easier downhill on
the way out) and follow the trail upward in a slightly strenuous
climb through the forest. The trail eventually ends at an old
township road. Hikers can take a spur trail not far along the road
to Green Mansions (clearly marked by a wooden sign), the
remnants of the Benua family's vacation home. After returning
from the side trail, hikers continue along the road, turning into a
dirt path at the dam and beautiful lake with hemlocks. Hikers
continue along the creek and meadows until returning to the fork
near the old homesite.

Benua Trail Map

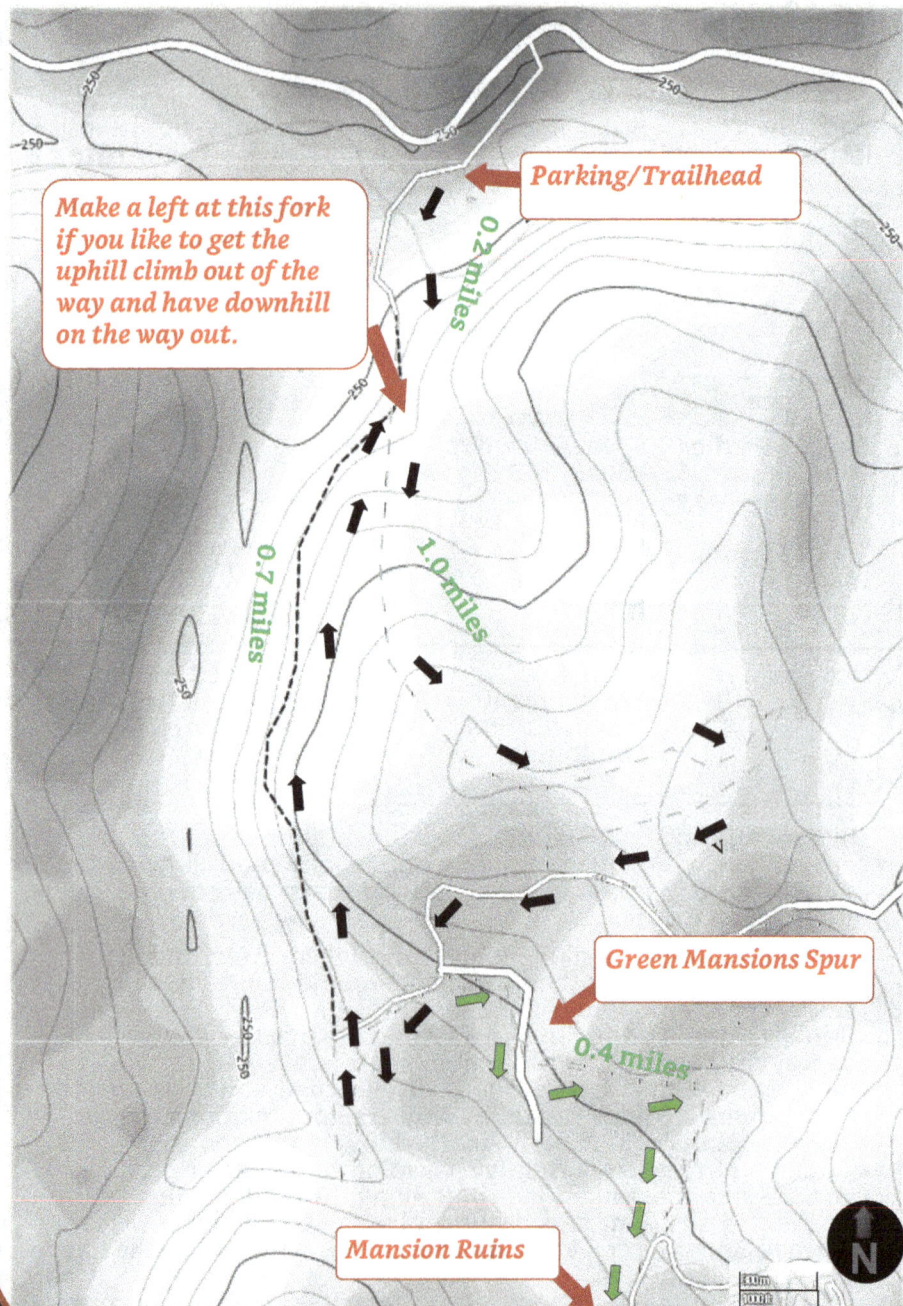

Parking/Trailhead

Make a left at this fork if you like to get the uphill climb out of the way and have downhill on the way out.

0.2 miles

0.7 miles

1.0 miles

Green Mansions Spur

0.4 miles

Mansion Ruins

N

Image: OpenStreetMap CyclOSM

Trailhead

Start/End Fork

Green Mansions Spur

Green Mansions, then (from nature sign on trail)

Green Mansions, now

87

State Nature Preserves

Shallenberger

Rhododendron Cove

Wahkeena

Christmas Rocks

Rockbridge

Boch Hollow

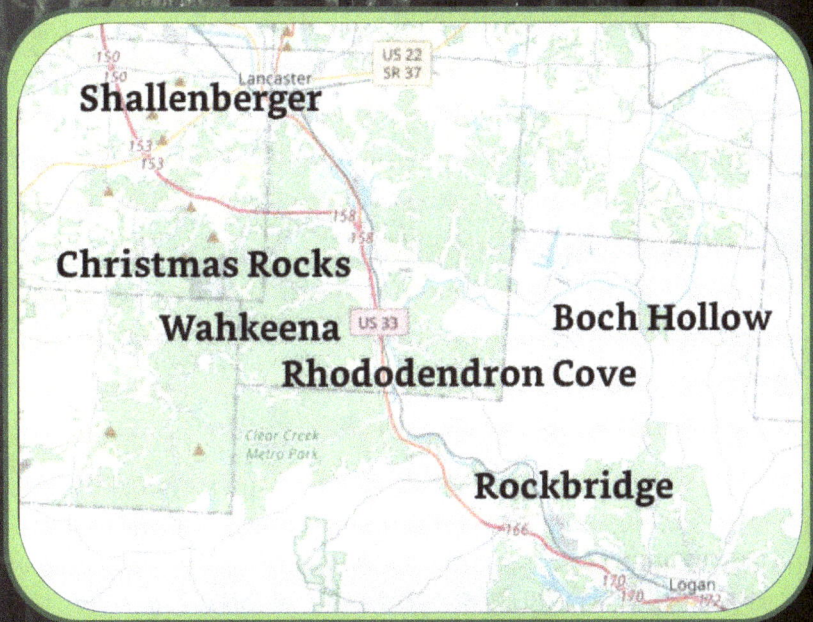

Shallenberger

Christmas Rocks

Wahkeena

Rhododendron Cove

Boch Hollow

Rockbridge

Shallenberger
State Nature Preserve
Allen and Ruble Knob Trail

Not far from Lancaster, two sandstone formations rise above the farmland surrounding them, named "knobs" by early settlers who saw them from below. Four nearby are Allen Knob, Beck Knob, Claypool Knob, and Ruble Knob. The 87 acres of Shallenberger Nature Preserve, named for Jay Shallenberger, who bestowed the parcel of land as a preserve, has Allen and the smaller Ruble knobs. Millions of years ago, sandy sediments were compressed at the bottom of the ocean covering this area. When the sea grew smaller, and the land was raised, the sandstone left behind created unique rock formations, outcroppings, and knobs. There is an old local legend of a hermit who lived in the region and who spent many hours atop Allen Knob looking out over the land. Before he died, he dug a grave atop the hill, and when he passed on, he was buried there. For many years, after his death, people would see his ghost coming down from Allen Knob and working his way along Beck Knob Road toward Hunter's Run. Once in a while, he would jump behind those riding horseback along the road and hitch a ride before disappearing!

Parking/Trailhead:

Shallenberger Nature Preserve
Allen and Ruble Knobs
2470 Becks Knob Rd SW
Lancaster, Ohio 43130
(39.691459, -82.657487)

Hike: Two loop trails are connected by a spur trail for a total 1.8 miles hike of both. Includes a side trail to Allen Knob. Hikers must stay on trail.

Type of Trail:	Quality:	Markings:
2 Loops 1 spur	*Nature Trail *Dirt path	**Blue**: Allen Knob (Blue Blazes on Trees) **Orange**: Ruble Knob (Orange Blazes)
Distance:	**Access:**	**Wheelchair Access:**
1.8 miles for both trails and spur to Allen Knob About 1 to 1.5 hours to hike.	*Open dawn to dusk/365 days a year. *No Dogs allowed	No
Restrooms:	**Features:**	**Parking GPS:**
No	Cliffs, Rock Formations	39.691459, -82.657487

This hike offers a gentle ascent through thick woodland and then rock formations and outcroppings. It has two loops connected by a short spur trail. The first loop has a side trail to Allen Knob and there is a stairway. The second loop skirts Ruble Knob.

Interesting sights include: Mountain laurel atop the knobs blooming in late spring and early summer. And, of course, the rocky outcroppings.

Allen/Ruble Knobs Trail Map

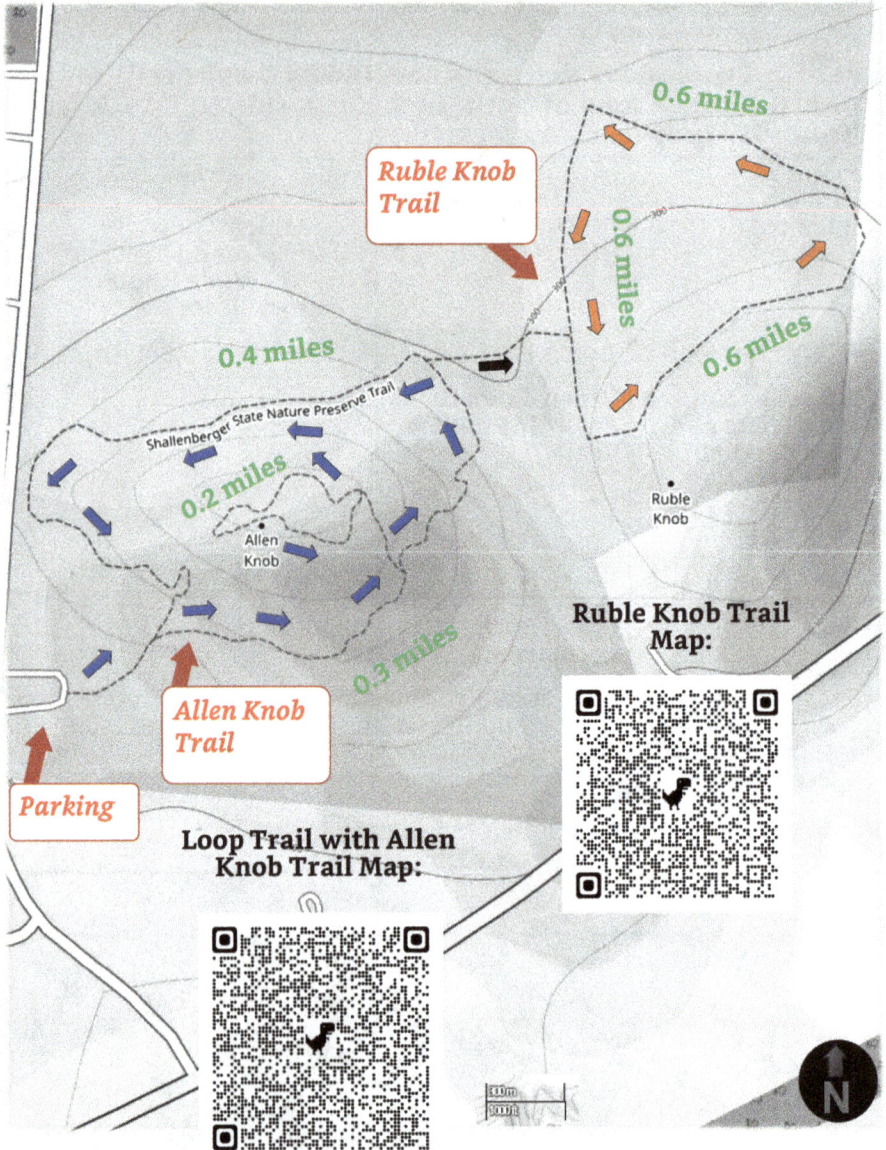

Ruble Knob Trail

0.6 miles

0.6 miles

0.6 miles

0.6 miles

0.4 miles

Shallenberger State Nature Preserve Trail

0.2 miles

0.3 miles

Allen Knob

Ruble Knob

Allen Knob Trail

Parking

Ruble Knob Trail Map:

Loop Trail with Allen Knob Trail Map:

Along the trail

Valley overlook

The trail

Rhododendron Cove State Nature Preserve

Rhododendron Cove Trail is described as a "magical place" even when the rhododendrons have yet to bloom (they are usually peak bloom in June) because the trail also offers huge unique rock formations and cliffs. It is about 75 acres.

Parking/Trailhead:

Rhododendron Cove State Nature Preserve
2730 Pump Station Rd SE
Lancaster, Ohio 43130
(39.631660, -82.558900)

Hike: **Moderately strenuous. Out and back trail/Loop. Starts and ends at a gravel parking area.**

Type of Trail:	Quality:	Markings:
Out and back with loops	*Developed Trail *Dirt path with cliffs	Orange: First Half (Orange Blazes on Trees) Blue: Second Half (Blue Blazes)
Distance:	**Access:**	**Wheelchair Access:**
Orange Trail: 1.2 miles Blue Trail: 1.9 miles Takes 1.5 to 2 hours to hike.	*Open dawn to dusk/365 days a year. *No Dogs Allowed	No
Restrooms:	**Features:**	**Parking GPS:**
No	Cliffs, Rock Formations, Seasonal flowers	39.631660, -82.558900 Watch for the Columbia Gas Crawford Compressor Station *on Pump Station Road*. The small, square gravel lot is across Pump Station Road (some GPS will lead you to a long driveway which is incorrect). Hikers can see the trailhead and kiosk at the end of a long fence line from the lot.

From the small gravel parking lot across from the compressor station, hikers can easily see the kiosk at the trailhead. After a short hike along a dirt path, the trail will ascend upward into the forest before coming to the tunnel-like rock formation. Hikers walk on the top of the hill, viewing cliffs, for a short loop (Orange blazes) or can continue onward for a second trail with a loop (blue blazes).

Interesting sights include: Watch for the pock-like holes on the sandstone walls, called "honeycomb weathering," because it resembles a bee's honeycomb.

The woody plants with the thick, waxy dark green leaves that flower in June are called rhododendrons. This preserve is believed to have the highest number of rhododendrons in Ohio.

Rhododendron Cove Trail Map

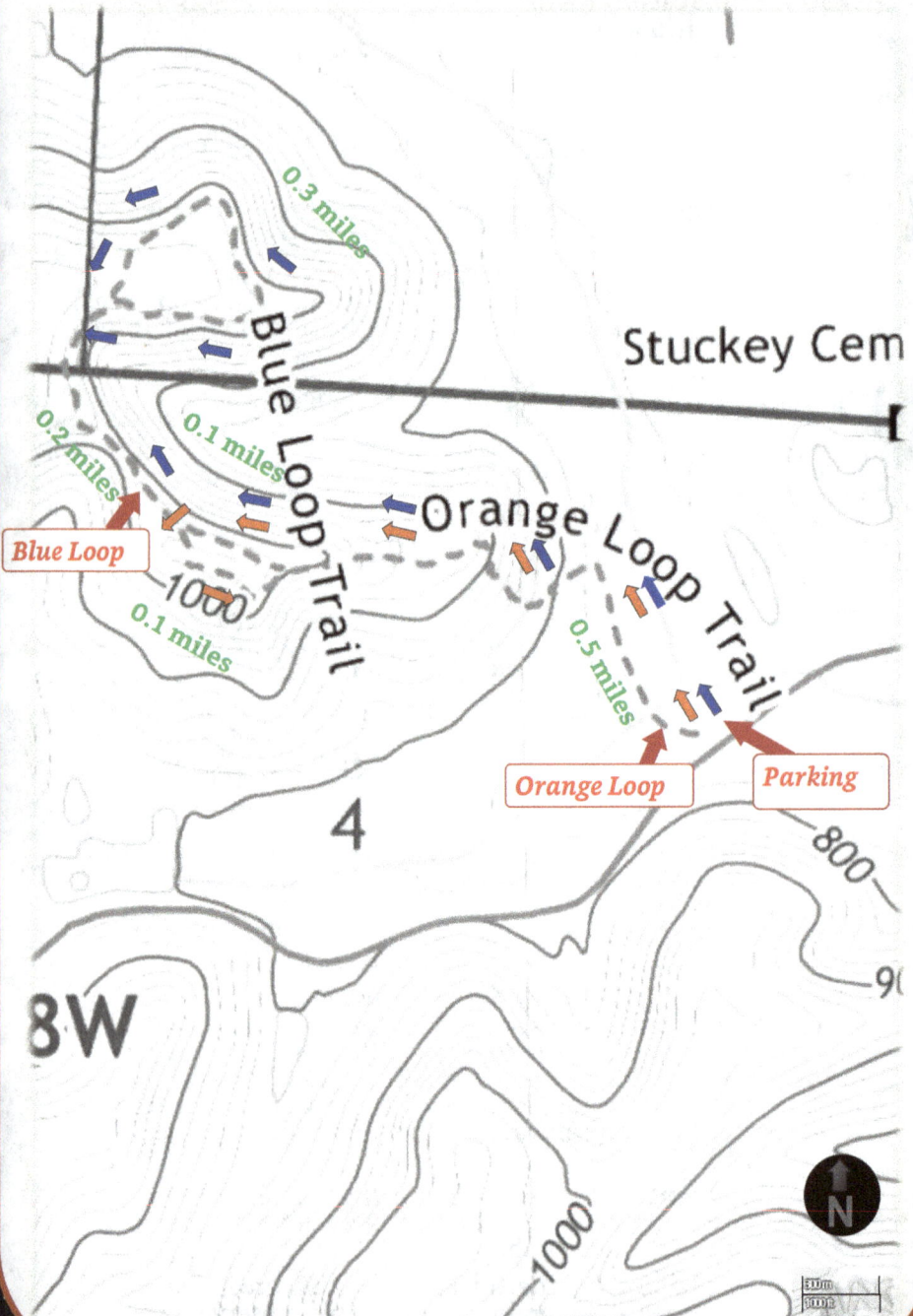

0.3 miles

Blue Loop Trail

Stuckey Cem

0.2 miles

0.1 miles

Blue Loop

Orange Loop Trail

0.1 miles

1000

0.5 miles

Orange Loop

Parking

4

800

90

8W

1000

N

Trailhead

Hilltop

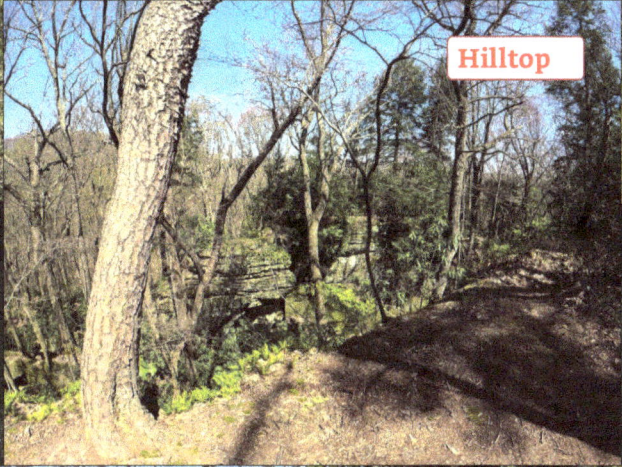
Along the trail

Wahkeena State Nature Preserve and Fairfield County Park District

2

Once farmland, the property was purchased by Doctor Frank Warner for his bride, Carmen, who was an avid gardener. She named it Wahkeena, meaning "most beautiful," in the Northwestern Native American Yakama tribe language. This 150-acre nature preserve is known for its flowers, like Showy Orchis and Pink Lady's Slipper, and its diverse wildlife. It has limited hours of operation.

Parking/Trailhead:
**Wahkeena State Nature Preserve/
Fairfield County Park District
2200 Pump Station Rd SE
Sugar Grove, Ohio 43155
(39.629640, -82.568920)**

Hike: Wahkeena Nature Preserve offers a variety of hiking trails and also a nature center. It is open seasonally and selected days of the week. Hikers must stay on trail.

Type of Trail:	Quality:	Markings:
Loop	*Nature Trail *Dirt path with steps/bridges	**Yellow**: Casa Burro (Yellow Blazes on Trees) **Brown**: Shelter Trail **Blue**: Pond Loop
Distance:	**Access:**	**Wheelchair Access:**
0.5 miles to 1.0 miles It takes about 1 to 2 hours to hike the trails.	*Hours and days open vary. *No Dogs Allowed	No
Restrooms:	**Features:**	**Parking GPS:**
Yes, near parking lot	Forest, Rock Formations, Nature Center with naturalists	39.629640, -82.568920

The main trails include:

Casa Burro: Named for Carmen Hambleton Warner's pet donkeys who were housed nearby, this trail is 1.0 miles long and makes its way through hilly forestland with beautiful rock formations before joining with the **Shelter Trail** for another .05 miles offering the same terrain.

Pond Loop: Loops around a small pond. 0.1 miles. Watch for spring wildflowers along the shore.

Boardwalk: A fun boardwalk weaves its way through another pond. Frogs are abundant in spring here. 0.1 miles.

Interesting sights include: A nature center offers information on natural history and has live animals.

Wahkeena Trail Map

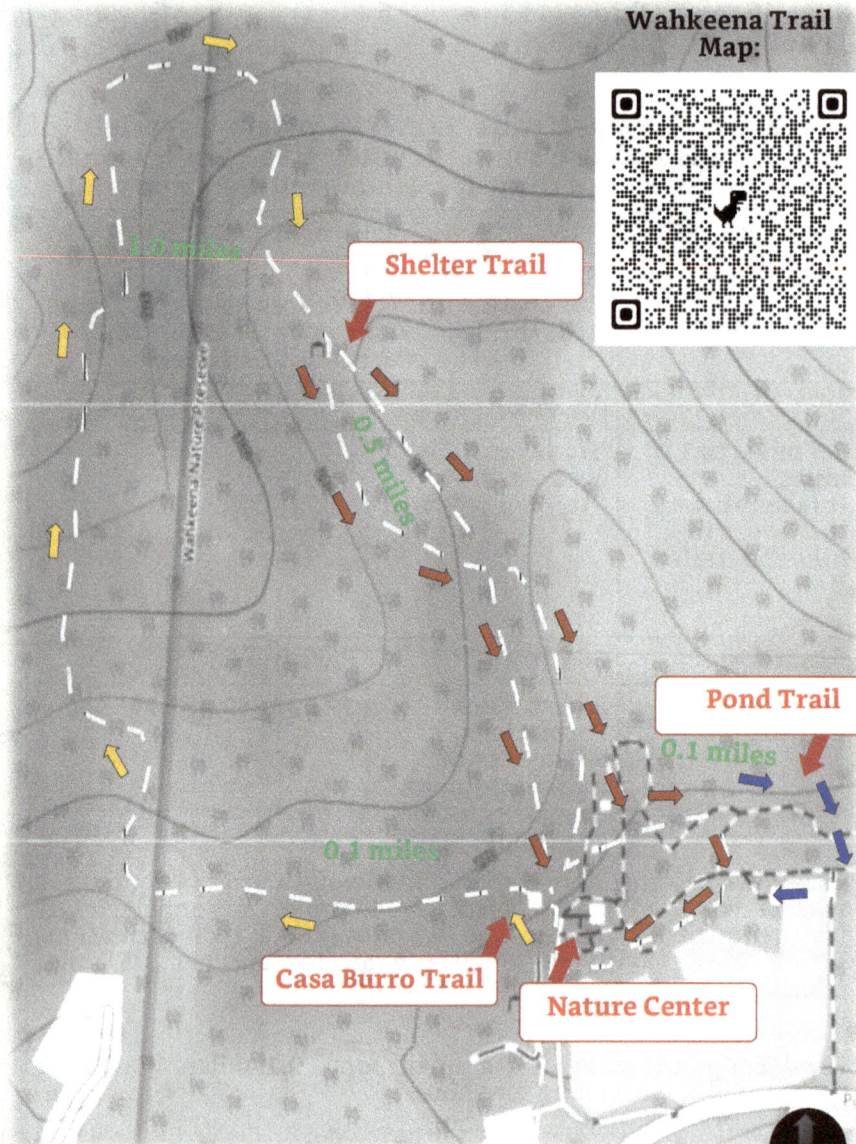

Wahkeena Trail Map:

Shelter Trail

1.0 miles

0.3 miles

Pond Trail

0.1 miles

0.1 miles

Casa Burro Trail

Nature Center

N

Image: OpenStreet Map CyclOSM

100 m
500 ft

Trailheads

Kiosk with updated maps and information

Boardwalk

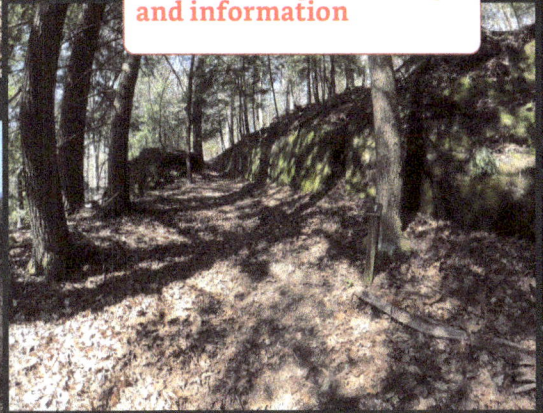

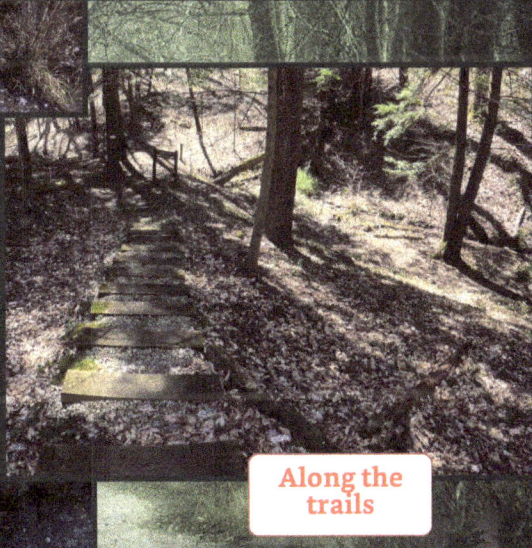

Along the trails

Christmas Rocks State Nature Preserve

Christmas Rocks State Nature Preserve, with its Black Hand Sandstone rock formations, offers a less crowded way to view the rugged and cliff-like character of the Hocking Hills. It is unclear how the preserve got its name, although some suggest it comes from the trees that look like Christmas pines growing along the crest of the ridge. Charles Goslin (local reporter, historian and naturalist for whom the park was originally named) suggested Jacobs Ladder, a high Black Hand Sandstone rock formation within the preserve, may have received its name from a local named Jacob Lader. He also relayed that the title may have come from settlers who noted the cliff stretches into the sky like Jacob's heavenly dream ladder in the Bible.

Parking/Trailhead:

Christmas Rocks State Nature Preserve
Intersections of Crooks Road SW, Meister
Road, and Old Mill Hollow Road
Lancaster, Ohio 43130
(39.639300, -82.649950)

Hike: The preserve offers two loop trails off the main trail—an Orange-blazed Loop many call Jacob's Ladder and a second Blue Loop. Hikers must stay on trail.

Type of Trail:	Quality:	Markings:
Out and back Loops	*Developed Trail *Dirt path with steps/bridges	Orange: Jacob's Ladder Overlook (Orange Blazes on Trees) Blue: Second Loop with rock formations (Blue Blazes)
Distance:	**Access:**	**Wheelchair Access:**
Orange Loop: 1.8 Blue Loop: 2.8 Both Loops: 3.4 2-3 hour hike.	*Open dawn to dusk/365 days a year. *No Dogs Allowed	No
Restrooms:	**Features:**	**Parking GPS:**
No	Overlook, Rock Formations	39.639300, -82.649950

Hikers start the trail at the Christmas Rocks Parking Lot kiosk next to Arney Run Park, following it along the gravel Old Mill Hollow Road. It is marked with posts along the roadway. The path continues as an old road before slimming to a dirt trail that parallels the gently flowing Arney Run.

Orange Loop: After 0.6 miles, hikers come to the "Jacob's Ladder" Loop Trail on the left. It is marked with orange blazes and is a strenuous climb upward. Once to the top, there is a pretty overlook view 250 feet over Arney Run. Hikers descend through the forest back to the main trail marked in orange blazes.

Orange Loop: Total out and back with orange-blazed loop trail is 1.8 miles.

Blue Loop: Hikers can continue just a short distance to a second loop marked by blue blazes and noted by a pole with a blue trail marker. The trail ascends upward through a forest and past rock formations, then works downward. Look upward to see a series of small recess caves along the way.

Trailhead to Blue Loop *without* Orange Loop: 2.8 miles.

Trailhead with both Blue Loop and Orange Loop: 3.4 miles.

Interesting sights along the way: Overlook and curious deer.

Christmas Rocks Trail Map

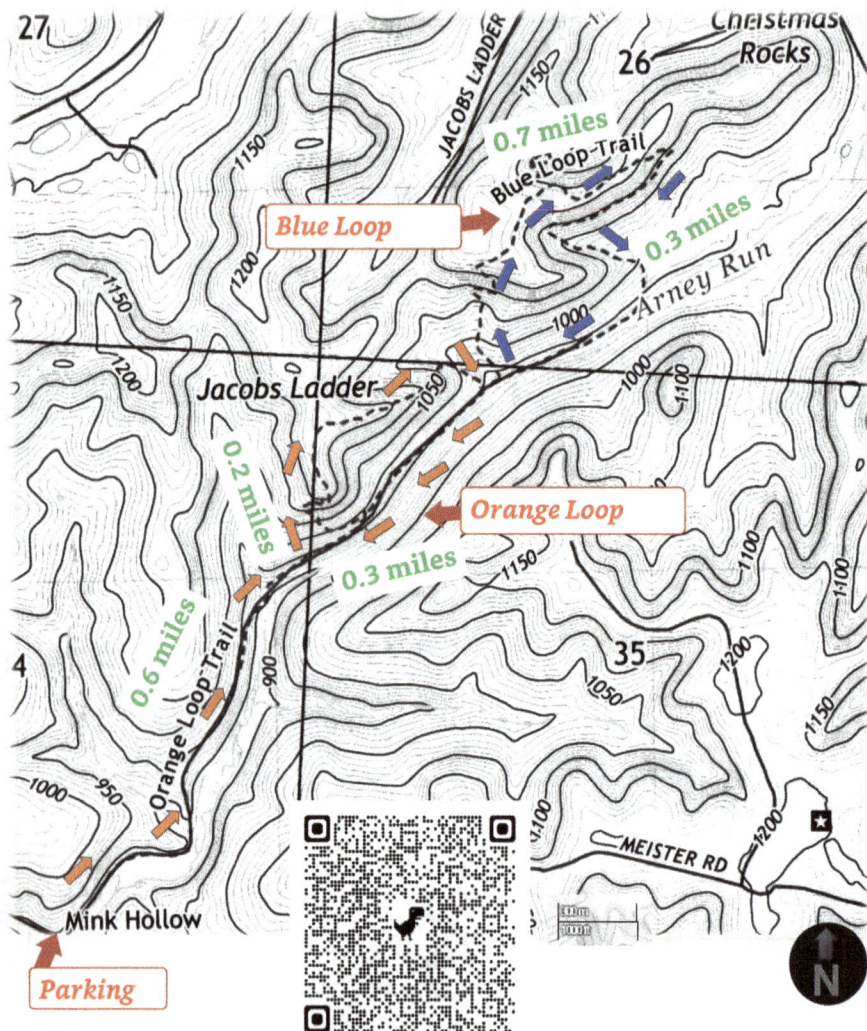

27

JACOBS LADDER

1150

26

Christmas Rocks

0.7 miles

Blue Loop Trail

1150

Blue Loop

1200

0.3 miles

1150

Arney Run

1000

1050

Jacobs Ladder

1200

0.2 miles

1000

1100

Orange Loop

0.3 miles

1150

1100

1100

1100

0.6 miles

Orange Loop Trail

900

35

1050

1200

1150

4

1000

950

1100

1200

1100

MEISTER RD

Mink Hollow

Parking

N

**Christmas Rocks
Trail Map: Orange
Loop with Jacob's
Ladder**

Trail continues

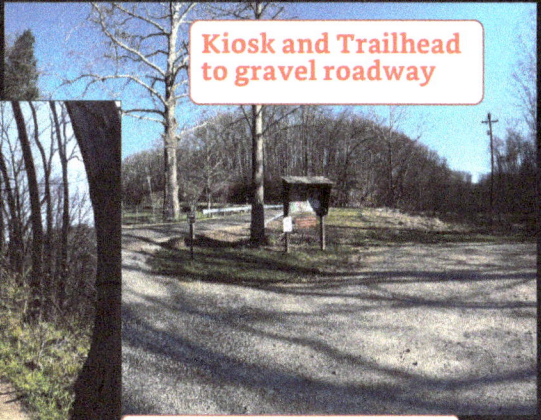
Kiosk and Trailhead to gravel roadway

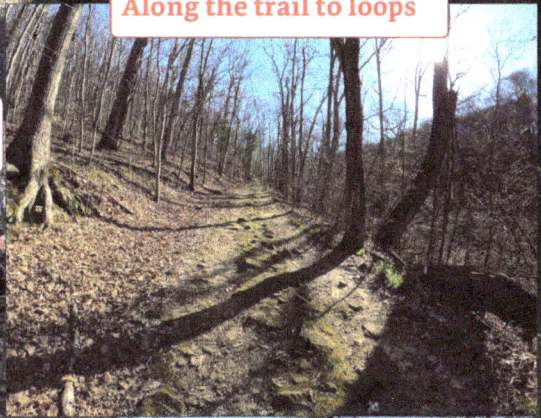
Along the trail to loops

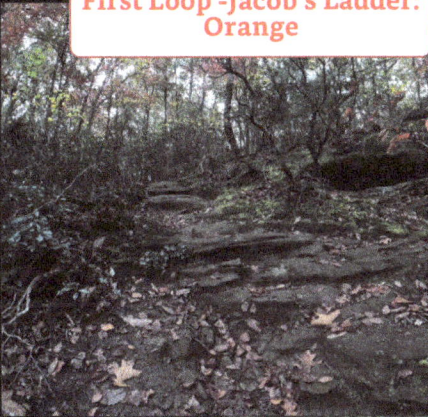
First Loop -Jacob's Ladder: Orange

Overlook on Orange Loop

Second Loop: Blue

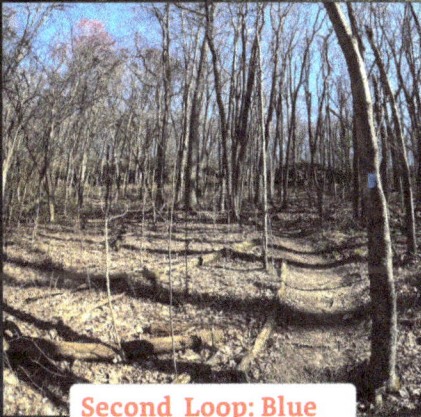
Along Blue Loop

Rockbridge State Nature Preserve

Rockbridge is a natural arch spanning more than 100 feet. It was made millions of years ago when Ohio was beneath an inland sea. As rivers flowed into this ocean, they brought sand that settled along the floor. With time, as more sand lay overtop it, it was packed down hard to make what is known as Black Hand Sandstone. Then, as the sea drained away years later, it left these layers exposed, and some began to erode over time, making the arch hikers see today.

Parking/Trailhead:
Rockbridge State Nature Preserve
11475 Dalton Road
Rockbridge, Ohio 43149
(39.566415, -82.499360)

Hike: There are 2.8 miles of trails with two loop trails, one displaying the natural rock bridge and the second, the rock shelter. Hikers must stay on trail.

Type of Trail:	Quality:	Markings:
Loop	*Developed trail *Dirt path	**Orange**: Natural Bridge Loop Trail
Distance:	**Access:**	**Wheelchair Access:**
Rock Bridge Trail: 1.6 miles Rock Shelter Trail: 1.5 miles Both together, 2.1 miles It takes about 1 to 2 hours to hike the trails.	*Open dawn to dusk/365 days a year. *No Dogs Allowed	No
Restrooms:	**Features:**	**Parking GPS:**
No	Cliffs, Rock Shelter, Rock Bridge	39.566415, -82.499360

Hikers start at the entrance trail at the parking lot ascending slightly upward along a rooted path and can take a loop with the natural rock shelter or natural rock bridge.

Interesting sights along the way: The rock bridge. Recess cave.

Rockbridge Trail Map

0.3 miles

0.2 miles

Rock Shelter Trail

Natural Bridge Loop Trail

0.3 miles

0.1 miles

0.2 miles

Rockbridge Trail Map:

0.5 miles

Natural Bridge Loop Trail

Dalton Road

Parking

Image: OpenStreetMap Tiles: Andy Allen

100 m
500 ft

The Rock Bridge

Along the trail

Boch Hollow State Nature Preserve

Boch Hollow, an area of thick forests, ponds, valleys, and ridges, was acquired by the Kessler family and donated as a preserve for hiking and educational opportunities for school children. It has diverse habitats and five trails – Cemetery, Meadow, Pond, Ridge, and a section of the Buckeye Trail.

Parking/Trailhead:

Boch Hollow State Nature Preserve
State Route 664
Logan, Ohio 43138

Hike: There are 3 trailheads with several options to hike the 7 miles of trails. Hikers must stay on trail.

Type of Trail:	Quality:	Markings:
Out and Back Loops	*Nature Trail *Dirt path with steps/bridges	Blue: Buckeye Trail
Distance:	**Access:**	**Wheelchair Access:**
7 miles of trails It takes about 1 to 4 hours to hike the trails.	*Open dawn to dusk/365 days a year. *No Dogs Allowed	No
Restrooms:	**Features:**	**Parking GPS:**
No	Forest, Rock Formations	39.633395, -82.418443 39.615130, -82.398343 39.627600, -82.431595

There are 3 trailheads with varied hiking trails including:
North Trailhead:
31893 Beach Camp Road Logan, Ohio 43138
(39.633395, -82.418443)
Buckeye Trail to Pond Loop Trail—1.7 miles: Hikers follow a spur trail at the parking lot and turn left at the blue blazed Buckeye Trail then a right on to the orange Pond Trail, making a loop after turning left back on to the Buckeye Trail, then right back to the parking lot spur.
East Trailhead:
7793 Bremen Road Logan, Ohio 43138
(39.615130, -82.398343)
Buckeye Trail to Cemetery Trail—2.8 miles: Hikers follow the blue blazes of the Buckeye Trail from the parking lot, then after 0.3 miles, turn right on to the green Cemetery Trail. Hikers will then make a left back on to the Buckeye Trail to return to the parking lot.
West Trailhead:
7100 State Route 664 Logan, Ohio 43138
(39.627600, -82.431595)
Buckeye Trail to Pond Loop Trail—2.9 miles: Hikers follow the blue blazes of the Buckeye Trail from the parking lot 1.1 miles to the orange Pond Trail, turning right. Then, by turning left when meeting with the Buckeye Trail, return to the parking lot.

Boch Hollow Trail Map

Pond Trail Map (via West Trailhead):

North Trailhead

Beach Camp Trail

0.3 miles

0.2 miles

0.3 miles

0.3 miles

0.9 miles

0.2 miles

0.4 miles

West Trailhead

Buckeye Trail

Cemetery Trail

0.7 miles

Pond Trail

0.5 miles

0.7 miles

0.7 miles

0.4 miles

0.4 miles

0.3 miles

0.4 miles

Cemetery Trail Map (via East Trailhead):

Parking – for Cemetery Trail

East Trailhead

Buckeye Trail (Out and Back 4.2 miles, one-way)

Cemetery Trail (Loop: 2.8 miles)

Pond Loop Trail—(Loop 1.7 miles)

North Trailhead Spur to Buckeye Trail

N

100 m
500 ft

Image: OpenStreet Map CyclOSM

Boch Hollow –Via East Trailhead - Cemetery Trail

Boch Hollow –Via West Trail - Pond Trail

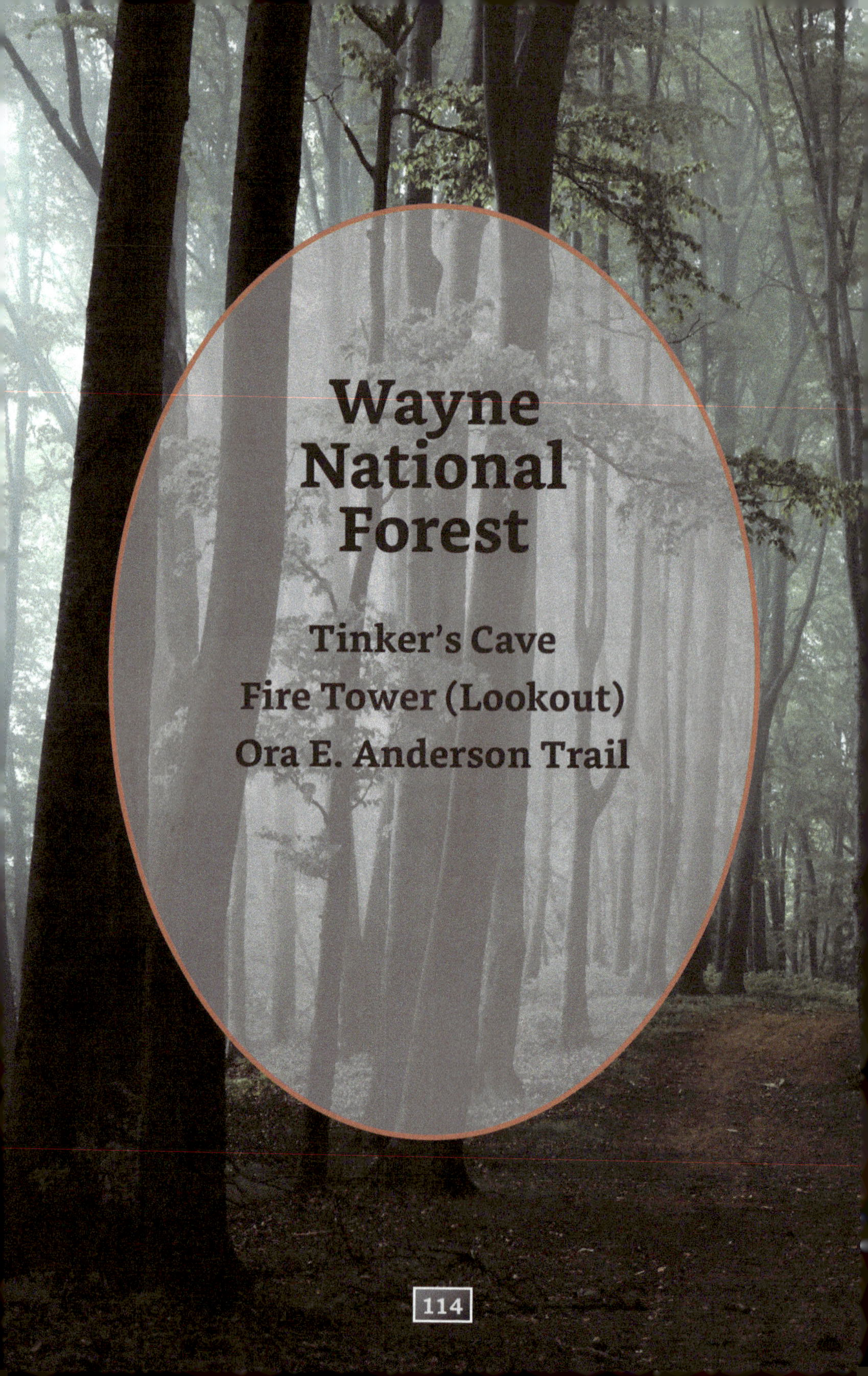

Wayne National Forest

Tinker's Cave

Fire Tower (Lookout)

Ora E. Anderson Trail

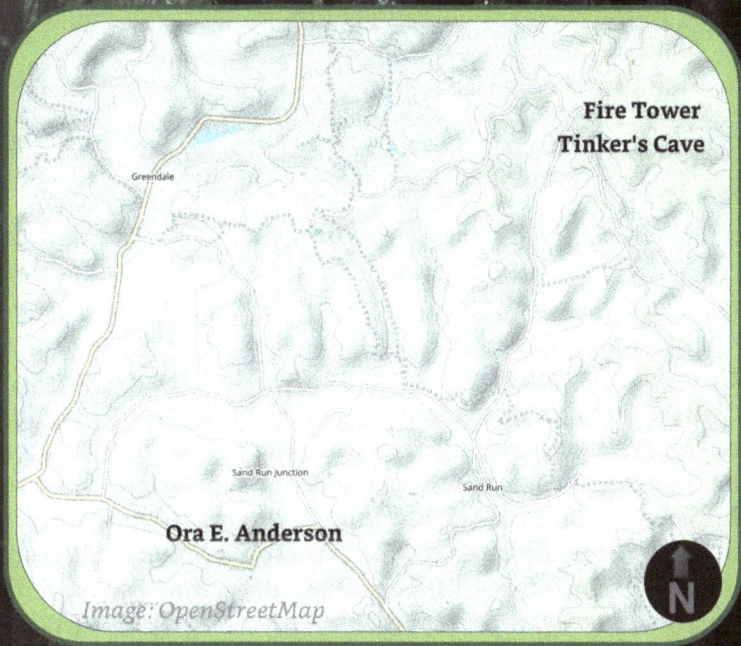

Fire Tower
Tinker's Cave

Greendale

Sand Run Junction

Sand Run

Ora E. Anderson

N

Wayne National Forest
Tinker's Cave

Shep Tinker lived in the area and was a horse thief and cattle rustler, hiding livestock in the region's caves until he could move them to northern Ohio to sell. He was always up to some mischief. One time, Tinker was riding through the country on a Sunday, and as he passed a church, he was mistaken for the circuit riding preacher arriving that morning. He was given a warm welcome, brought into the church, preached a sermon, and was on his way soon after without anyone knowing the better! Once, he stole a black horse belonging to a local doctor. Upon seeing Tinker sneak off with his horse, the doctor took off after the thief and nearly caught up. Realizing he would be overtaken, Tinker bound the horse's muzzle with a white cloth and turned the horse around until he was heading toward the doctor. In the darkness, the man called out to Tinker and asked if he had seen a rider with a black horse. Tinker said, "Yes, I did! He went thataway!" He pointed the poor physician in the direction he had come. The doctor took off again after his horse, not realizing until later the horse thief had tricked him! Shepherd Tinker disappeared after the Civil War. Locals always said that Shep stole horses from the wrong farmer and ended up on the short end of a noose right in the cave where he hid most of his stolen animals and the large rock shelter that bears his name, Tinker's Cave. Some say Tinker and his stolen horses haunt it!

Parking/Trailhead:
Wayne National Forest
12318 Burton Hill Road
New Straitsville, Ohio 43766
(39.545483, -82.226367)

Hike: This rugged out and back trail takes hikers to the legendary cave of a long-dead horse thief. There is also a a side hike to a historical fire lookout tower from the 1930s.

Type of Trail:	Quality:	Markings:
Out and Back	*Trail	No
Distance:	**Access:**	**Wheelchair Access:**
0.2 miles, one way. The path is steep and rugged to the cave. It takes a half hour to hike.	*Open dawn to dusk/365 days a year. *Well-behaved dogs on leash allowed.	No
Restrooms:	**Features:**	**Parking GPS:**
No	Recess Cave	39.545483, -82.226367

For parking, watch for the small gravel pull-off on Burton Hill Road. Hikers take the rugged trail on the same side as the pull-off, down the hillside to the cave and can return along the same path. Or continue up the small hill on the right (with back to cave) in front of the cave along the path (watch the boundary marker for private property) to the top of the hill and Sand Run Road. Take a right on the roadway watching for traffic, then turn right on the next road, Burton Hill Road, to return to the vehicle.

Hike: 0.2 miles, one way. Out and back. The path is steep and rugged to the cave (39.544650, -82.227180).

Side Hike: Just a short walk up the road is the historical **Shawnee Fire Tower**, built by the Civilian Conservation Corps in 1939. Although hikers can no longer scale its height, they can stop in for a visit. It is 100 feet tall! 0.1 mile, one way. Out and back.
Payne Cemetery—Along the drive, travelers may pass a small cemetery on State Route 595 tucked on a narrow ridgetop. It is almost all that remains of the small farming and mining community of Paynes Crossing, once a population of freed African Americans. In the mid-1800s, the community was spread out over the countryside and was involved in the Underground Railroad Movement. There is a pull-off to visit the cemetery: (39.56148, -82.257964)

Tinker's Cave Trail Map

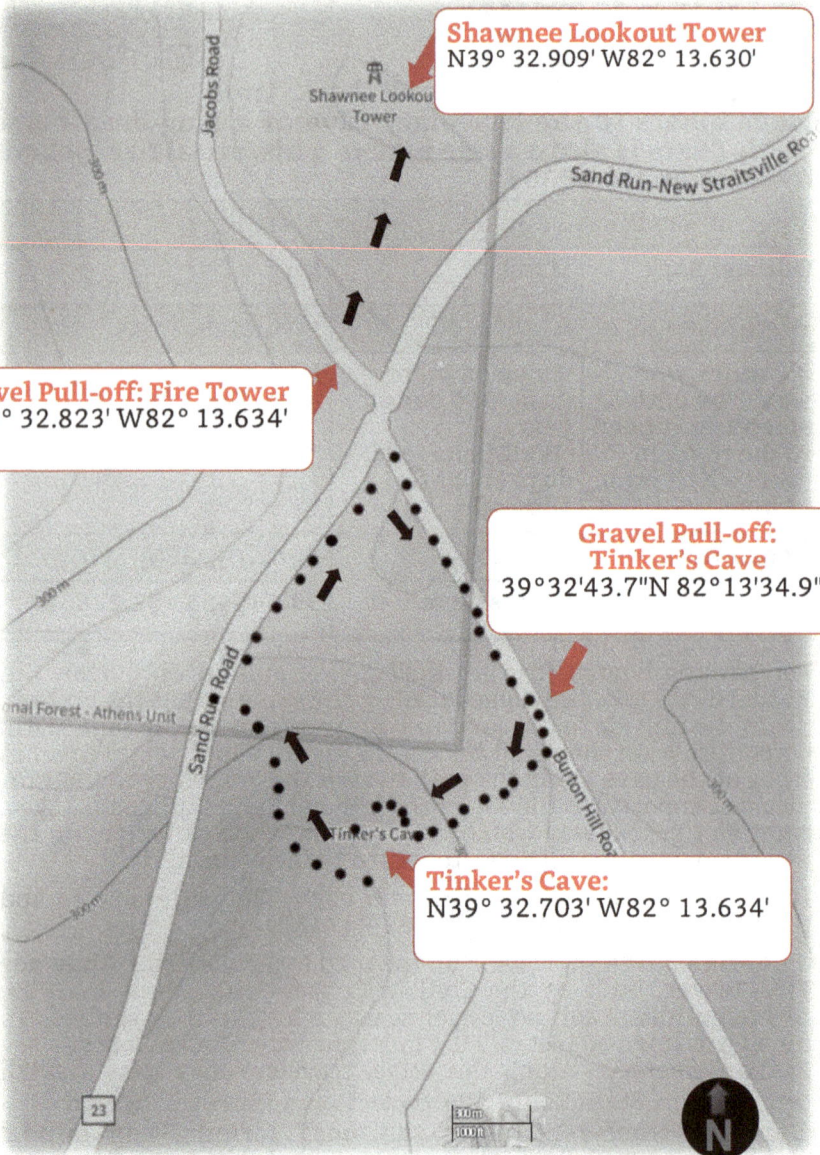

Shawnee Lookout Tower
N39° 32.909' W82° 13.630'

Gravel Pull-off: Fire Tower
N39° 32.823' W82° 13.634'

**Gravel Pull-off:
Tinker's Cave**
39°32'43.7"N 82°13'34.9"W

Tinker's Cave:
N39° 32.703' W82° 13.634'

Jacobs Road

Sand Run-New Straitsville Road

Sand Run Road

Burton Hill Road

National Forest - Athens Unit

Shawnee Lookout Tower

Tinker's Cave

23

300 m
1000 ft

N

Openstreet Maps

118

Tinker's Cave

Along the trail

Shawnee Lookout Tower

Wayne National Forest
Ora E. Anderson Trail

The Ora E. Anderson Trail works its way through a wetland filled with wildlife such as beavers, deer, reptiles, and amphibians. It is a hotspot for birders, with over 60 bird species identified in surveys. It features a kiosk with interpretive information in addition to nature signs along the trail with poetry by nature writer and conservationist Ora E. Anderson and illustrative watercolor artwork by Barbara Sheriff Kostohryz of Athens.

Parking/Trailhead:
Wayne National Forest
Ora E. Anderson Nature Trail
OH-278
Carbon Hill, Ohio 43111
(39.510202, -82.261290)

Hike: Out and back nature trail on an old rail bed embraced by wetlands of the Monday Creek Bottoms, a pine forest, pond, and hardwood forest. Offers a kiosk with interpretive information and nature signs along the trail with poetry by Ora E. Anderson.

Type of Trail:	Quality:	Markings:
Out and Back	*Nature Trail *Rail-trail	Interpretive signage
Distance:	**Access:**	**Wheelchair Access:**
0.5 miles, one-way. About a half hour.	*Open dawn to dusk/365 days a year. *Well-behaved dogs on leash allowed.	No
Restrooms:	**Features:**	**Parking GPS:**
No	Wetland, interpretive signs	39.510202, -82.261290

The trail is an out-and-back nature trail on a railbed section of the Columbus and Hocking Valley Railroad. Hikers park in the designated lot and follow a grassy path paralleling State Route 278 to the trailhead. The path is embraced by the Monday Creek Bottoms wetlands, a pine forest, a pond, and a hardwood forest. The hike is 0.5 miles, one-way. Wear a hunter-orange vest if coming in the fall and winter during the hunting season. In spring and summer, insect repellent is recommended.

Interesting sights along the way: Beavers have made their home here and are credited with creating this wetland by damming a culvert once draining a nearby field. You can see their dens around the marsh.
Watch for the old concrete railroad markers along the trail.

Ora E. Anderson Trail Map

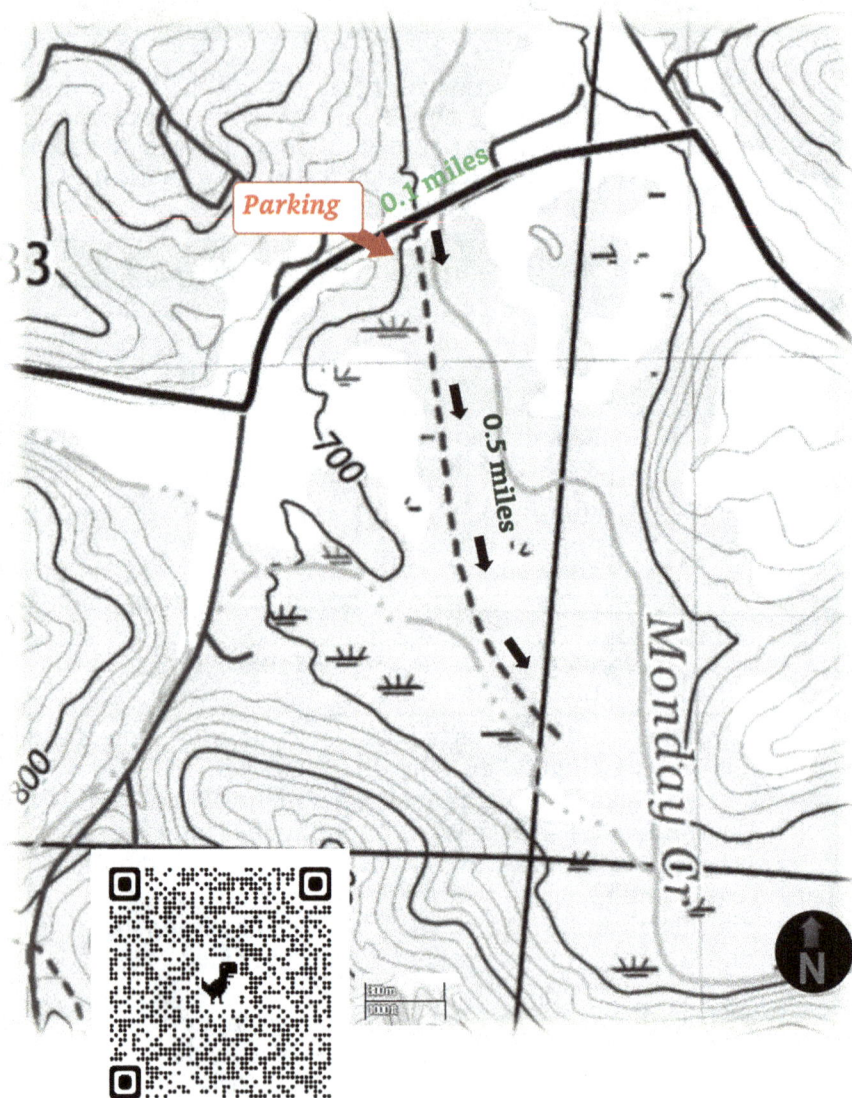

Parking

0.1 miles

0.5 miles

700

800

33

Monday Cr

N

Ora E. Anderson
Trail

Trailhead

Along the trail

Hidden Jewels With Limited Parking

**Twin Falls &
Chapel Cave
(Hocking State Forest)**

**Big Springs & Balanced Rock
(Devil's Tea Table)
(Hocking State Forest)**

**Airplane Rock
(Hocking State Forest)**

Twin Falls

Chapel Cave

Airplane Rock

Conkle's Hollow

Balanced Rock

Big Springs

Image: OpenStreetMap

N

Hocking State Forest
Twin Falls & Chapel Cave

Twin Falls and Chapel Cave are a couple of hidden wonders accessed by a small parking area near Conkle's Hollow. Most overlook this trail as it is part of the Hocking State Forest Bridle Trail system, but foot traffic is welcome. The trail is a bit rugged and fun—hikers cross a couple small creeks and can clamber over fallen logs and rocks to get here. It can be muddy. However, the seasonal waterfalls pouring down the high rock cliff at Twin Falls are breathtaking, and the trail is typically not as crowded. The cathedral-like Chapel Cave, also known as 21 Horse Cave, was supposed to fit twenty-one horses within its immense interior. It is along a side trail near Twin Falls.

Parking/Trailhead:

Hocking State Forest
Twin Falls & Chapel Cave (21 Horse) Trail
Rock Climbing/Rappelling Lot
24798 Big Pine Road
Logan, OH 43138
(39.458883, -82.558475)

Hike: The trail is 2.2 miles total along a horse bridle trail and creek leading to seasonal waterfalls and a side loop to visit Chapel Cave and high cliff faces.

Type of Trail:	Quality:	Markings:
Out and Back	*Multi-use Trail Bridle & Hiking	Yes, Orange blazes for bridle, Blue for Buckeye. White for side trail to Twin Falls/Chapel Cave
Distance:	**Access:**	**Wheelchair Access:**
2.2 miles, takes about 1.5 hours to hike	*Open dawn to dusk/365 days a year. *Well-behaved dogs on leash allowed.	No
Restrooms:	**Features:**	**Parking GPS:**
Closest are at Conkle's Hollow Parking Lot.	Cave, cliffs, waterfalls	39.458883, -82.558475

The trail begins at the end of the rock climbing and rappelling parking lot. The gravel lot holds about 50 cars. Hikers follow a bridle trail (Orange Blazes) and Buckeye Trail (Blue Blazes) and then the Chapel Cave/Twin Falls Trail (White Blazes) through the forest and along a shallow creek that is easily traversable and crosses the path several times.

After leaving the parking lot, hikers continue straight where the bridle trail intersection "0" enters to the left (N39° 27.622' W82° 33.545'). Hikers resume along the dirt/mud trail until the next waymark where the horse trail, marked with an orange arrow, goes right (N39° 27.946' W82° 33.595'). Follow the trail straight, and a small sign states: **Chapel Cave**. The blazes, afterward, will be white, which hikers will follow until the trail ends at Twin Falls (N39° 28.248' W82° 33.524'). (Hikers will pass the loop trail that leads to Chapel Cave on the right) Return to the path for Chapel Cave and make a loop, passing Chapel Cave (N39° 28.091' W82° 33.501') around back to the main trail. Return along the same route.

Interesting sights along the way: Meandering creek, cliffs, rock formations, waterfalls, and a unique cave.

Twin Falls & Chapel Cave Trail Map

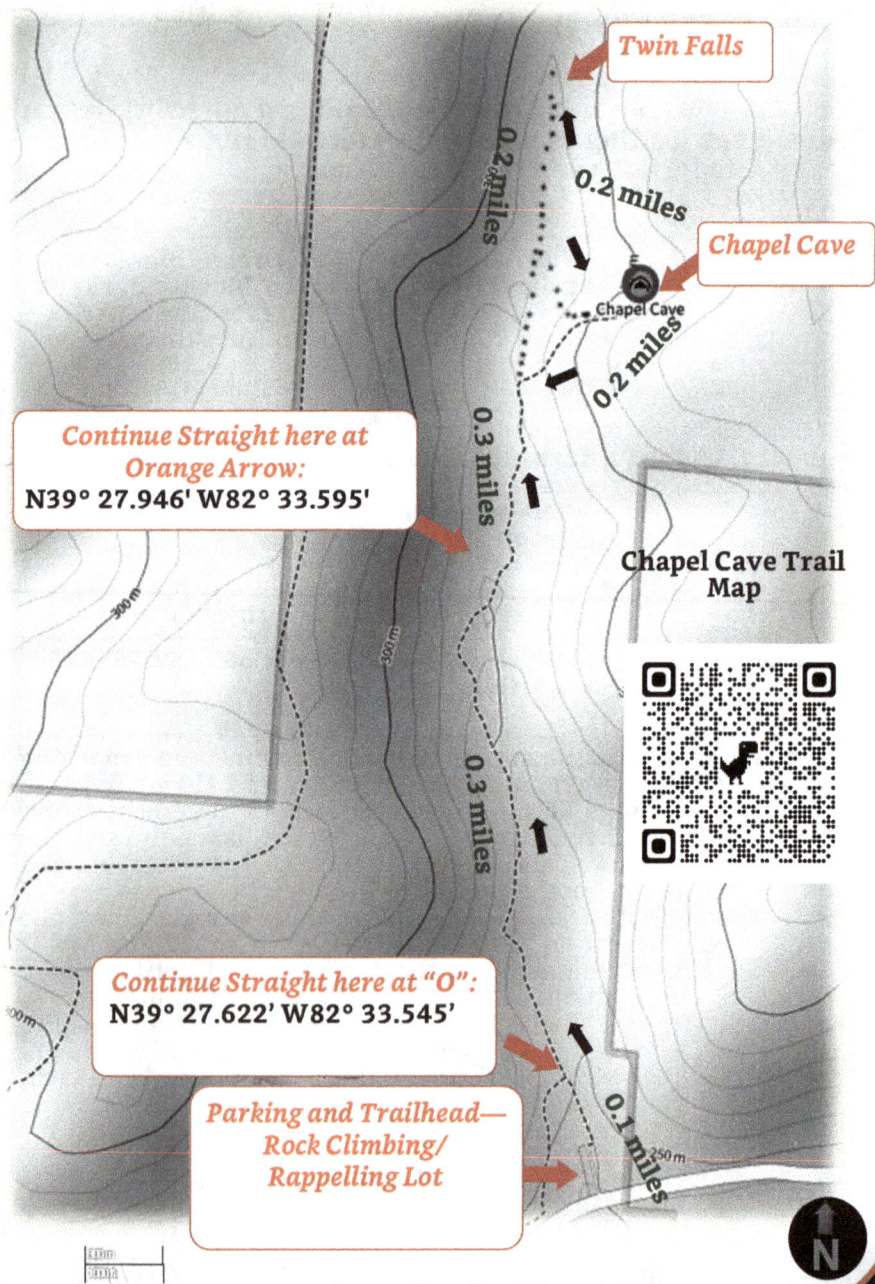

Twin Falls

0.2 miles

0.2 miles

Chapel Cave

Chapel Cave

0.2 miles

Continue Straight here at Orange Arrow:
N39° 27.946' W82° 33.595'

0.3 miles

Chapel Cave Trail Map

0.3 miles

Continue Straight here at "O":
N39° 27.622' W82° 33.545'

0.3 miles

Parking and Trailhead— Rock Climbing/ Rappelling Lot

0.1 miles

Image: OpenStreetMap

The first intersection of the trail. At "0", go straight. Follow the Orange (Bridle Trail) and Blue (Buckeye Trail) Blazes.

Small white sign just past creek shows white trail to cave and waterfalls.

Bridle Trail Arrow. Bridle trail goes right.

Twin Falls

Chapel Cave

Hocking State Forest

Big Spring Hollow Falls & Balanced Rock

The two separate trails for Big Spring Hollow Falls and Balanced Rock can be accessed by crossing Big Pine Road from the same parking area (Rock Climbing and Rappelling lot) as Chapel Cave (21 Horse Cave) and Twin Falls. The trailheads are easily seen from the parking lot.

Big Spring Hollow offers a short hike through a hemlock forest and along a bubbling stream ending in a picturesque waterfall. Big Spring Hollow Waterfall is 120 feet tall, and believed to be the tallest known year-around waterfall in Ohio.

Hikers can follow a separate path to Balanced Rock, a tall, naturally occurring sandstone pillar known as Devil's Tea Tables. The area of the Hocking Hills began eroding millions of years ago; over time, the sandstone bedrock began to wear down. But sandstone is a loose conglomerate (mixture) of layered hard and soft materials. The rock balanced on top is a harder seam of sandstone than the base. The base or pillar holding it is a looser conglomerate easily eroded by water, creating the illusion of a balanced stone on top.

Parking/Trailhead:
Hocking State Forest
Big Springs/Balanced Rock Trails
Rock Climbing/Rappelling Lot
24798 Big Pine Road
Logan, OH 43138
(39.458883, -82.558475)

Hike: Big Spring is a short hike via a meadow, then deep Forest to the waterfall. Hikers taking the trail to Balanced Rock can explore the area of a unique geological feature.

Type of Trail:	Quality:	Markings:
Out and Back	*Multi-use Trail *Bridle/Hiking	Balanced Rock: Blue Blazes: Buckeye Trail/ Big Springs: None
Distance:	**Access:**	**Wheelchair Access:**
Big Spring Hollow: 0.6 miles one-way (20 minutes) Balanced Rock:0.6 miles, one-way (about 45 minutes)	*Open dawn to dusk/365 days a year. *Well-behaved dogs on leash allowed.	No
Restrooms:	**Features:**	**Parking GPS:**
Closest are at Conkle's Hollow	Tea Table, Waterfall	39.458883, -82.558475

After parking at the lot, hikers will **walk across Big Pine Road** to the rock climbing and rappelling area. After passing the kiosk and going over the bridge, there is a registration kiosk (for climbers) and three trails starting at the same point: **The left trail leads to Balanced Rock**. **The right leads to Big Springs Hollow Falls**. The center trail leads to the rock climbing and rappelling area. (Trailhead: N39° 27.489' W82° 33.456')

Big Springs Hollow Falls: After crossing the bridge, hikers will take the **trail to the right** through a meadow and then a hemlock forest. It ends at the waterfall. Hike is 0.6 miles one-way, 1.0 mile total. Easy. (Waterfall Waypoint: N39° 27.179' W82° 33.641')

Balanced Rock: After crossing the bridge, hikers **will take the trail to the left,** following the blue blazes of the Buckeye Trail and ascending to the lower level of the rock climbing and rappelling area, an enormous cliff area. Hikers then cross through two large cuts in the rock. As the trail turns, hikers will note wooden horse posts along the path. It is here, when turning slightly, there is a clear view of Balanced Rock. Uphill climbs. Easy to moderate. (Balanced Rock Viewing Waypoint: (N39° 27.437' W82° 33.120') It is 0.6 miles, one-way, total of 1.0 miles.
Interesting sights along the way: The tallest known waterfall in Ohio. A unique geologic feature known as a Devil's Tea Table.

Big Spring Hollow Falls & Balanced Rock Trail Map

Parking and Trailhead—Rock Climbing/Rappelling Lot for both trails

Balanced Rock Trail Take Trail to Left Blue Blazes

Balanced Rock

0.3 miles

Big Spring Hollow Trail Take trail to right

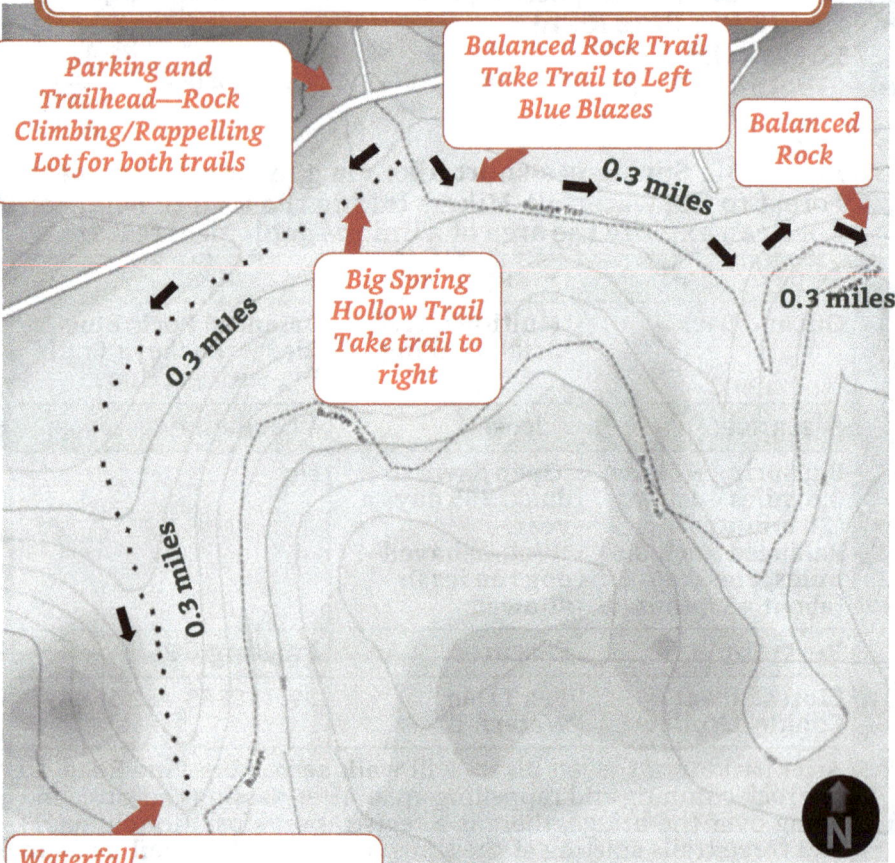

0.3 miles

0.3 miles

0.3 miles

N

Waterfall:
Waterfall Waymark:
N39° 27.179' W82° 33.641'

Big Springs Hollow Falls Waypoint:

Balanced Rock Map from parking area to Balanced Rock:

Image: OpenStreetMap

Kiosk *after* crossing the bridge over Pine Creek.

To rock climbing area

To Balanced Rock

To Big Springs Hollow Waterfall

Balanced Rock

Big Springs

Hocking State Forest
Airplane Rock
(and side trail to Chapel Cave and Twin Falls)

The hike to Airplane Rock, a rock outcropping shaped like the nose of a plane, in Hocking State Forest is a true treat away from the crowds. The trail, forested on either side, is along an old, well-maintained service road, and the Hocking Bridle Trail goes up and down the hills with a side trail well-marked with a sign.

An added side trail along the old service road (maps and images are following the Airplane Rock map and images) is an alternate route to Chapel Cave (21 Horse Cave) and Twin Falls.

Parking/Trailhead:

Hocking State Forest
17741 Hockman Road
Rockbridge, OH 43149
(39.473326, -82.555351)

Hike: Hikers take a service road up and down hills surrounded by forest along the Hocking Forest Bridle trail to a rock formation called Airplane Rock. And a side trail to Chapel Cave/Twin Falls.

Type of Trail:	Quality:	Markings:
Out and Back	*Multi-use Trail *Bridle/Hiking	*Airplane Rock: Bridle Trail Orange Blazes – *Chapel Cave/Twin Falls: Orange/White
Distance:	**Access:**	**Wheelchair Access:**
*Out and back 1.8 miles, one way. About 1.5 to 2.0 hours. *Chapel Cave/Twin Falls side trail: 1.8 miles 1.5 hours	*Open dawn to dusk/365 days a year. *Well-behaved dogs on leash allowed.	No
Restrooms:	**Features:**	**Parking GPS:**
*Outhouse only before Airplane Rock only	Airplane Rock Side Trail: Chapel Cave/Twin Falls	39.473326, -82.555351

The trailhead for both trails is beyond the orange service gate at the far end of the gravel parking area. Hikers will walk 0.3 miles following the blue blazes of the Buckeye until an intersection at a curve (N39° 28.314' W82° 33.534').

Hikers heading to Airplane Rock will continue **following the old road to the right** and heed **the orange Bridle Trail blazes** between beautiful hemlock forests. There is a sharp veer along the road with a wooden outhouse, horse tie-offs, and an easily visible sign marking the short side trail to Airplane Rock (N39° 27.669' W82° 34.010'). The trail is 1.8 miles, one-way, out and back, easy to moderately strenuous for the hills.

Hikers heading on the side trail to Chapel Cave/Twin Falls will turn left, following the **blue blazes of the Buckeye Trail**. The trail weaves through the forest along the cliffs. The trail turns right off the Buckeye Trail at a sign marked "No Horses," located at waymark: (N39° 28.065' W82° 33.513') and descends to an outcropping and then works slightly upward to Chapel Cave (N39° 28.091' W82° 33.501'). Hikers continue the path, descending to the creek. **Turning right** along the trail marked with white blazes (N39° 28.078' W82° 33.499'), hikers will end at Twin Falls. (N39° 28.248' W82° 33.524') The trail is 1.8 miles, one-way, out and back, easy to moderately strenuous for the hills.

Interesting Sites: Airplane Rock, Chapel Cave, Twin Falls.

Airplane Rock Trail Map

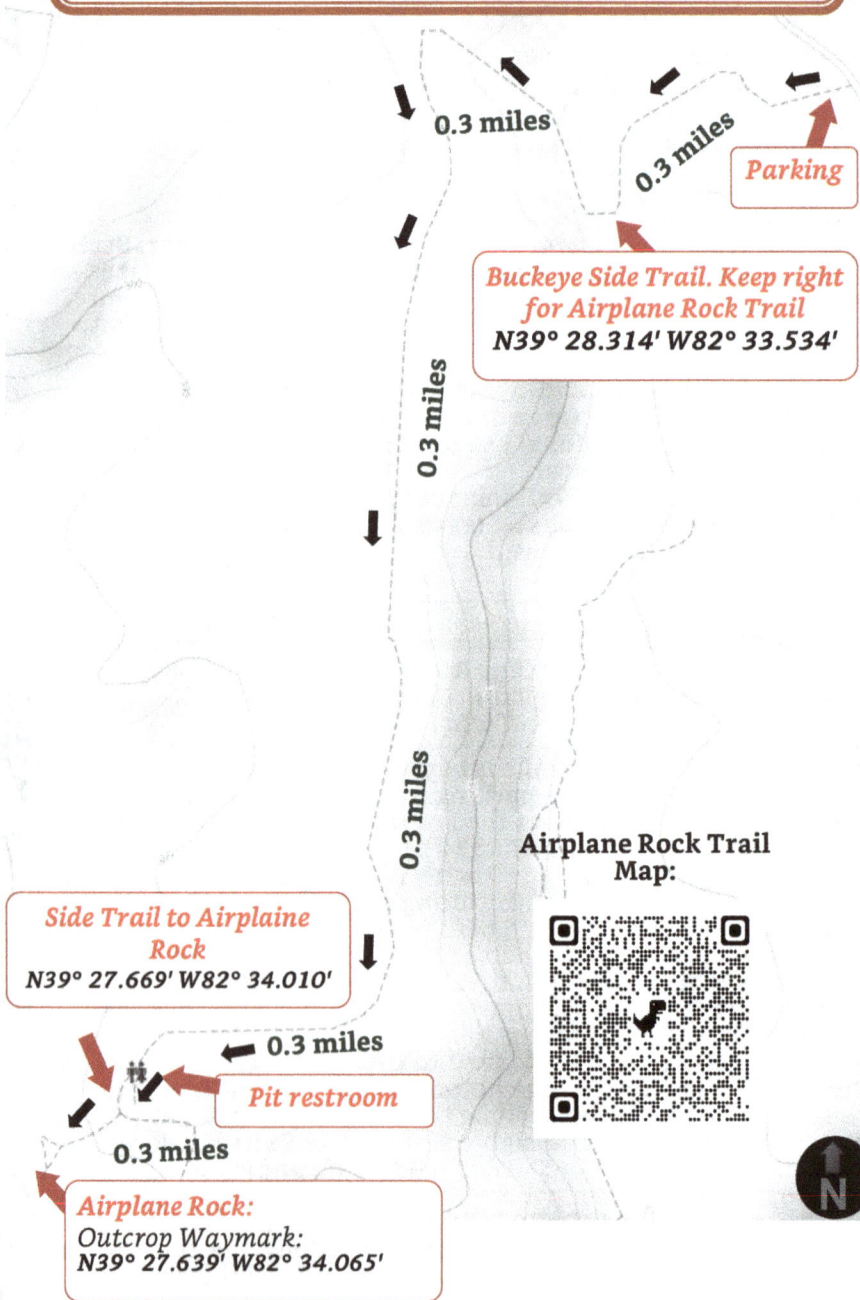

0.3 miles

0.3 miles

Parking

Buckeye Side Trail. Keep right for Airplane Rock Trail
N39° 28.314' W82° 33.534'

0.3 miles

0.3 miles

Airplane Rock Trail Map:

Side Trail to Airplaine Rock
N39° 27.669' W82° 34.010'

0.3 miles

Pit restroom

0.3 miles

Airplane Rock:
Outcrop Waymark:
N39° 27.639' W82° 34.065'

N

Image: OpenStreetMap : Andy Allan

Trailhead at end of Parking

Buckeye Trail continues here with blue blazes (and orange for turn in bridle trail)

Continue to the right on the gravel road to Airplane Rock— Orange Blazes

Orange blazes and restroom. Side trail directly after.

Trail sign at turn after restroom

Airplane Rock

Side Trail off Airplane Rock Trail to Chapel Cave/Twin Falls Trail Map

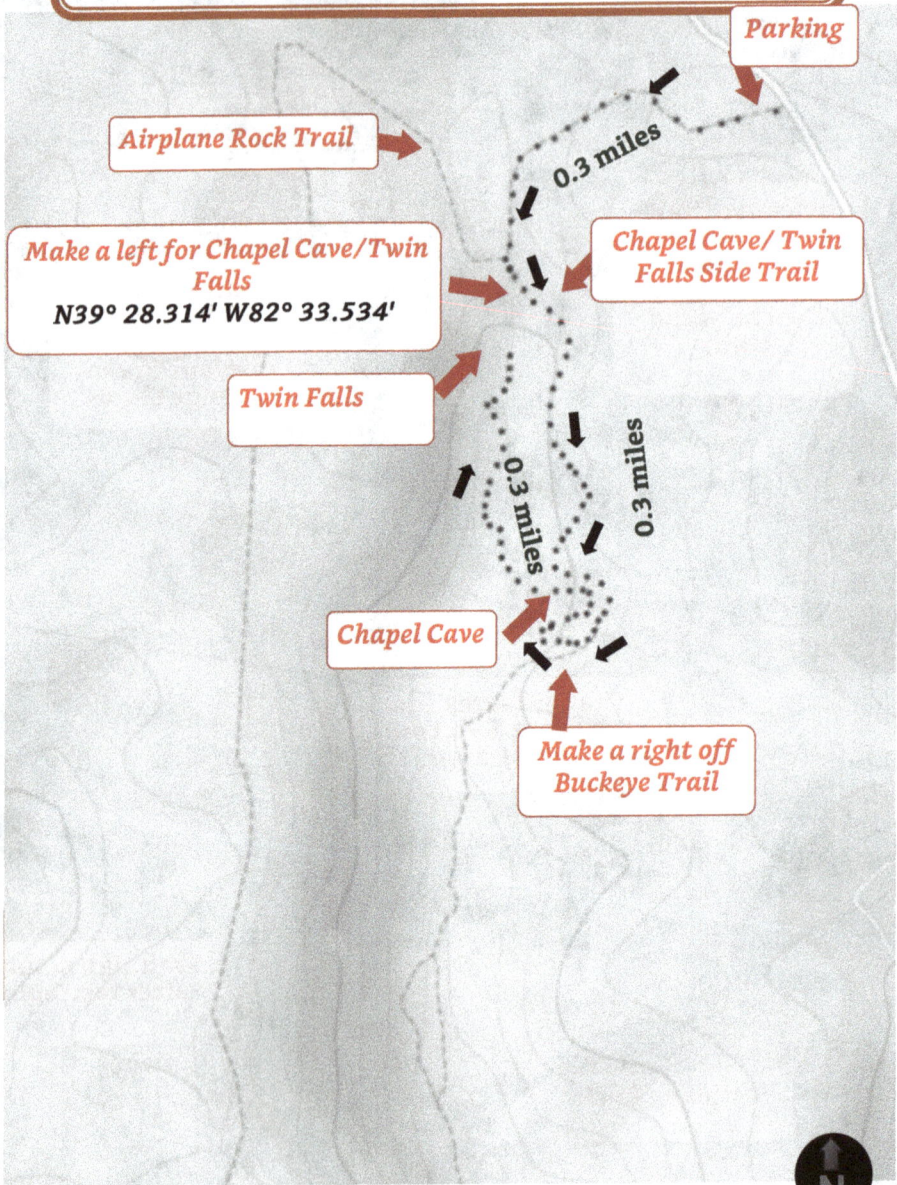

Parking

Airplane Rock Trail

0.3 miles

Make a left for Chapel Cave/Twin Falls
N39° 28.314' W82° 33.534'

Chapel Cave/ Twin Falls Side Trail

Twin Falls

0.3 miles

0.3 miles

Chapel Cave

Make a right off Buckeye Trail

N

Trailhead at end of Parking

Take this left continuing along the Buckeye Trail with blue blazes (and orange for turn in bridle trail)

This way along the gravel road goes to Airplane Rock—Orange Blazes

Orange and blue blazes along the trail.

Twin Falls

Chapel Cave

Short Drives Away

Lake Katharine
(Ohio State Nature Preserve
in Jackson, Ohio)

Hock-Hocking Adena Hike
and Bikeway
(Nelsonville/Athens, Ohio)

Hocking Hills State Park

Athens Hockhocking Adena
Hike/Bike

The Plains

Athens

Lake Katharine

Jackson

Image: OpenStreetMap

N

Lake Katharine
State Nature Preserve
Jackson County

About an hour's drive from Old Man's Cave, Lake Katharine was once Camp Arrowhead, a boys' summer camp operated from 1949 to 1965. In 1975 Edwin Jones and James McKittrick donated the land to the state, establishing it as a nature preserve. The preserve was named after Jones's wife, Katharine. Although part of the land was mined for coal in the 1800s, the 2000-acre property has several undisturbed, deep Appalachian ravines, a man-made lake, and over 5 miles of trails.

Parking/Trailhead:
Lake Kathrine Hiking Parking lot
Lake Katharine Road
Jackson, OH 45640
(39.086046, -82.669602)

Hike: The Salt Creek Loop trails are two of the five distinct trails at the nature preserve. Others include: Calico Bush, Lakeview, and Pine Ridge. All are accessed at the same parking area.

Type of Trail:	Quality:	Markings:
Loops	*Nature Trails	Yes, signs
Distance:	**Access:**	**Wheelchair Access:**
0.5 to 2.0 miles Each takes 0.5 to 1 hour to hike	*Open dawn to dusk/365 days a year. *No Dogs Allowed	No
Restrooms:	**Features:**	**Parking GPS:**
Yes, outhouse	Rock formations, stream, ravines	39.086046, -82.669602

Salt Creek Long Loop
Notable with the trails at Lake Katharine is that they intersect at certain points, allowing hikers to explore more areas and add distance to their hike.

Hikers start the trail from the parking area at the sign designating "TRAIL ENTRANCE: SALT CREEK SHORT LOOP, SALT CREEK LONG LOOP," which will take them along the Salt Creek Short Loop 0.2 miles until it intersects with the longer loop. The path for the Salt Creek Long Loop is taken to the right about a mile through forests of birch, beech, and hemlock, along Salt Lick Creek, then through deep ravines. After, it intersects with the Salt Creek Short Loop once again for 0.2 miles. Then hikers can take: Pine Ridge Trail to the left 0.3 miles back to the parking area *Or* Take Pine Ridge Trail to the right for a short jaunt to where it intersects with Calico Bush Trail. Calico Bush Trail is to the left. It is 0.5 miles to Pine Ridge Trail where hikers turn left (At this juncture, hikers can add two separate loop trails – Lakeview Trail –1.1 miles or Pine Ridge Trail—2.0 miles) for 0.1 miles back to the parking area.

Lake Katharine Trails:
· Calico Bush Trail - 0.5 miles, about .5 hours
· Lakeview Trail - 1.1 miles, about 1 hour
· Pine Ridge Trail - 2 miles, about 1.5 hours
· Salt Creek Short Loop - 0.6 miles, about .5 hours
· Salt Creek Long Loop - 1.1 miles, about 1 hour
Due to high water, there may be seasonal closures of Lakeview and Pine Ridge Trail.

Lake Katharine Trail Map

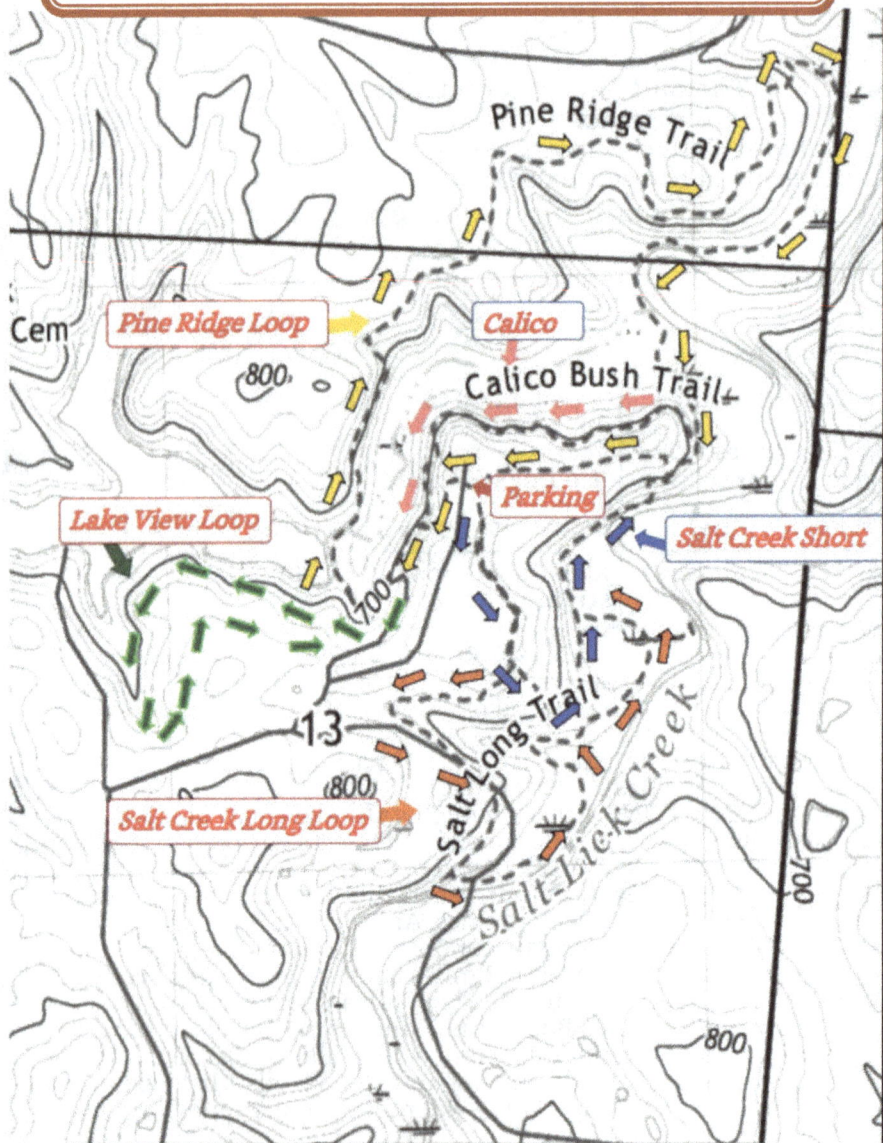

Pine Ridge Trail

Pine Ridge Loop

Calico

Calico Bush Trail

Cem

800

Parking

Lake View Loop

Salt Creek Short

700

Salt Long Trail

13

Salt Lick Creek

(800)

Salt Creek Long Loop

700

800

N

Trailheads at parking area-easy to find.

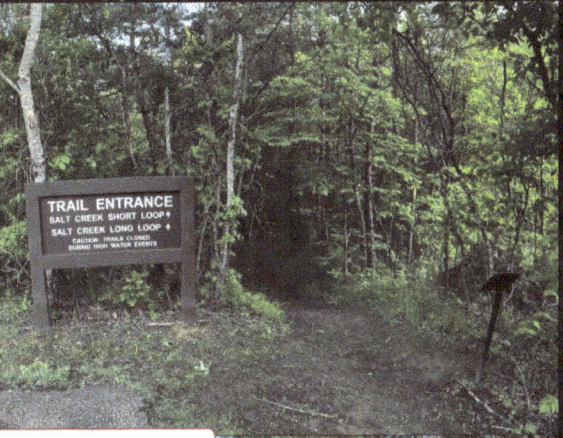

TRAIL ENTRANCE
SALT CREEK SHORT LOOP
SALT CREEK LONG LOOP
CAUTION: TRAILS CLOSED
DURING HIGH WATER EVENTS

TRAIL ENTRANCE
PINE RIDGE
CALICO BUSH
LAKEVIEW

Along the Trails

Hockhocking Adena Bikeway

The Columbus and Hocking Valley Railroad stretched from Columbus to Nelsonville by 1869 and, within another year, reached Athens; its main loads were that of the abundant coal found within the region. It is this old railroad bed that communities eventually developed into over 21 miles of hike-bike trail called the Hockhocking Adena Bikeway. The trail runs from Athens to Nelsonville along a level and smooth asphalt surface past Hocking College's Robbins Crossing Pioneer Village and through small towns, forests and preserves, countrysides, and even the Hocking River. Partway, it passes the old mining community of Hocking, sitting atop Eclipse Mine #4. The Eclipse Company Store was renovated into a restaurant along the bike trail and is a favorite stop of both hikers and bikers and is about 10.9 miles from the trailhead in Nelsonville.

Parking/Trailhead:

**Hockhocking Adena Bikeway Trailhead
(Rocky Outdoor Gear Store)
Myers Street
Nelsonville, Ohio 45764
(39.457642, -82.231290)**

Hike: A 1.7 miles, one way section of the 21.0 miles Hockhocking Adena Bikeway takes hikers along a rail-trail to Robbins Crossing Historical Village and Hocking College Nature Center.

Type of Trail:	Quality:	Markings:
Out and Back	*Rail Trail *Multi-use Trail	Yes, signs
Distance:	**Access:**	**Wheelchair Access:**
1.7 miles from Rocky Boots to Hocking College Robbins Crossing and Nature Center	*Open dawn to dusk/365 days a year. *Well-behaved dogs on leash allowed.	Yes
Restrooms:	**Features:**	**Parking GPS:**
Rocky Boots Hocking College Visitor Center	Historical buildings, nature center	39.457642, -82.231290

The trail begins at Rocky Boots parking lot by making a left along the route. The old railroad bed weaves its way through part of town, past historic trains in the process of being renovated, then crosses the Hocking River. Hikers follow the path in front of Hocking College before seeing Robbins Crossing Historical Village on the left and then Hocking College Nature Center, offering Appalachian Ohio natural history information, native animals, and birds of prey and mammal programs. Both are open for special events, daily visits, and weekly programming.
Interesting sights along the way: Robbins Crossing Historical Village and Hocking College Nature Center. Rocky Boots.

Hockhocking Adena Bikeway Trail Map

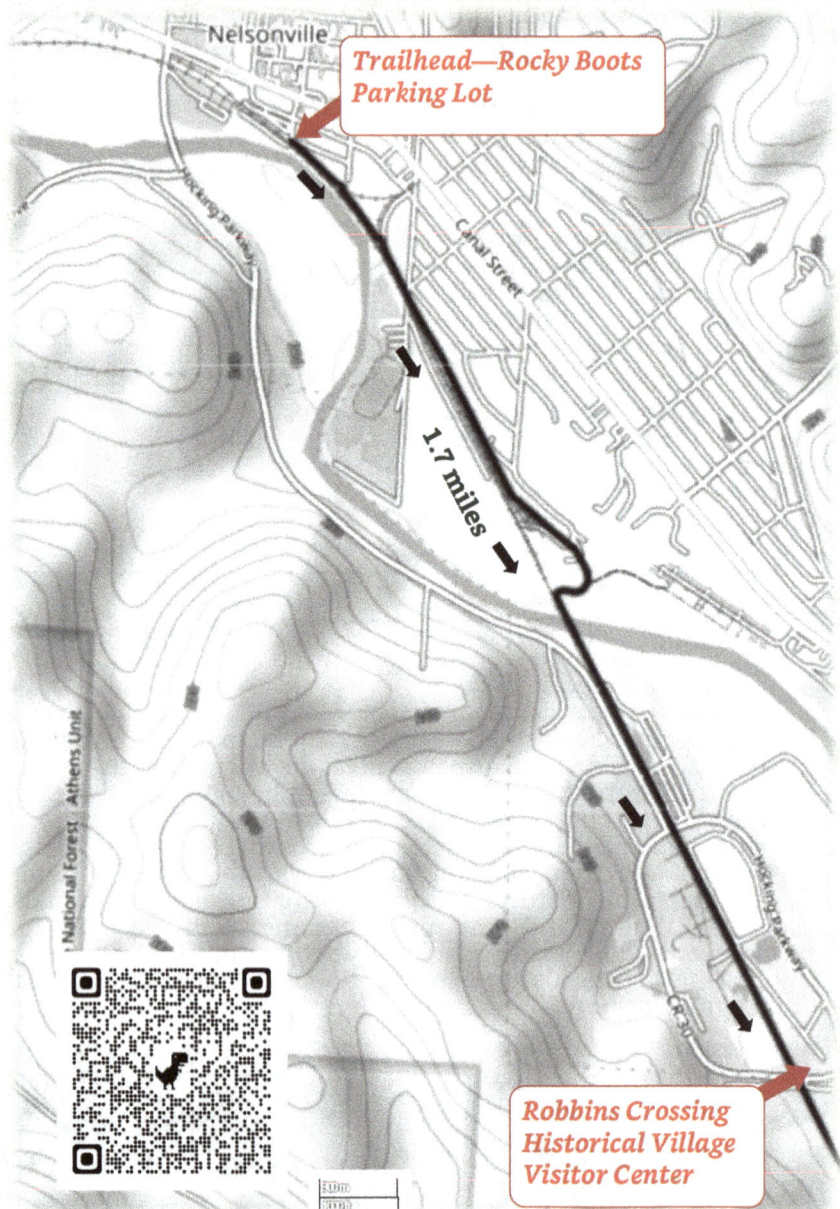

Trailhead—Rocky Boots Parking Lot

1.7 miles

Robbins Crossing Historical Village Visitor Center

Hockhocking Adena Hike/Bike Trail to Robbins Crossing Map:

Image: OpenStreetMap

Along the trail

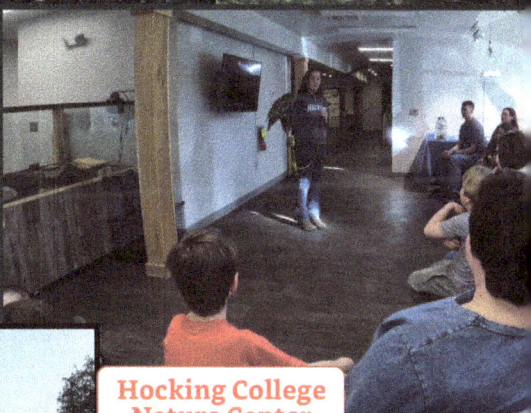

Robbins Crossing

Hocking College
Nature Center

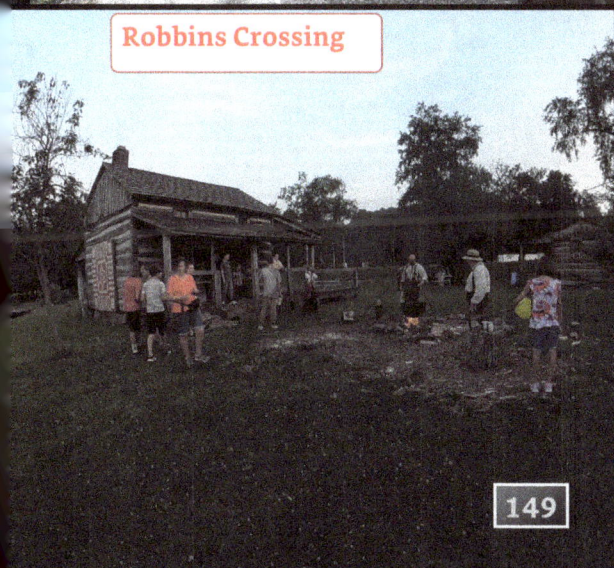

149

ODNR State of Ohio Nature Preserves in the Hocking Hills
by Permit Only

Permits are free, but hikers must apply online 14 days in advance by contacting: Ohio State Nature Preserves Access Permit:

ohiodnr.gov/buy-and-apply/special-use-permits/nature-preserve-access

Upon approval, the windshield parking permit and hiking permits along with trail information and physical locations are sent by the agency.

*Boch Hollow: Laurel Falls

*Sheick Hollow

*Little Rocky Hollow

Bock Hollow: Laurel Falls

State Nature Preserve

Area: Boch Hollow near Logan, Ohio. Permit Only! No dogs. There is a very short trail across the roadway from the gravel lot, then a staircase to an observation platform to view the falls.

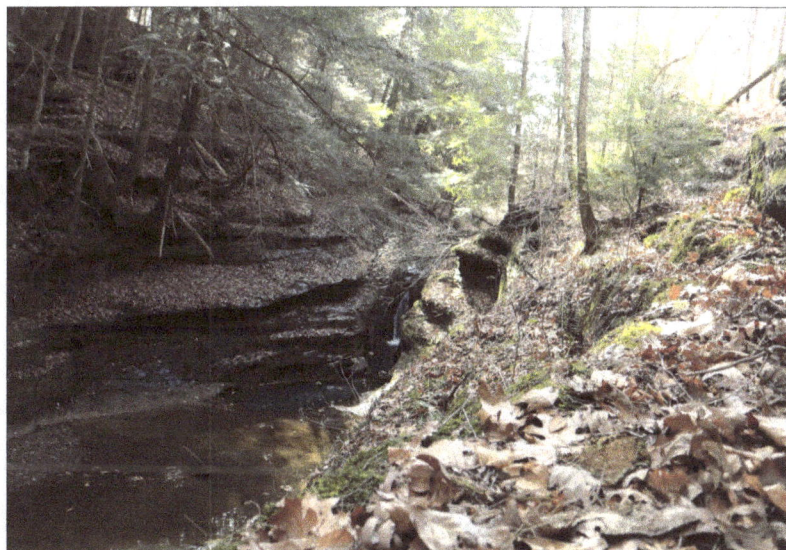

Sheick Hollow State Nature Preserve

State Nature Preserve

Area: Near Conkle's Hollow Permit Only! No dogs.

There is a short entrance trail marked with orange blazes from the small gravel parking lot through a hemlock forest and then along a creek. Thereafter, there is no official trail.

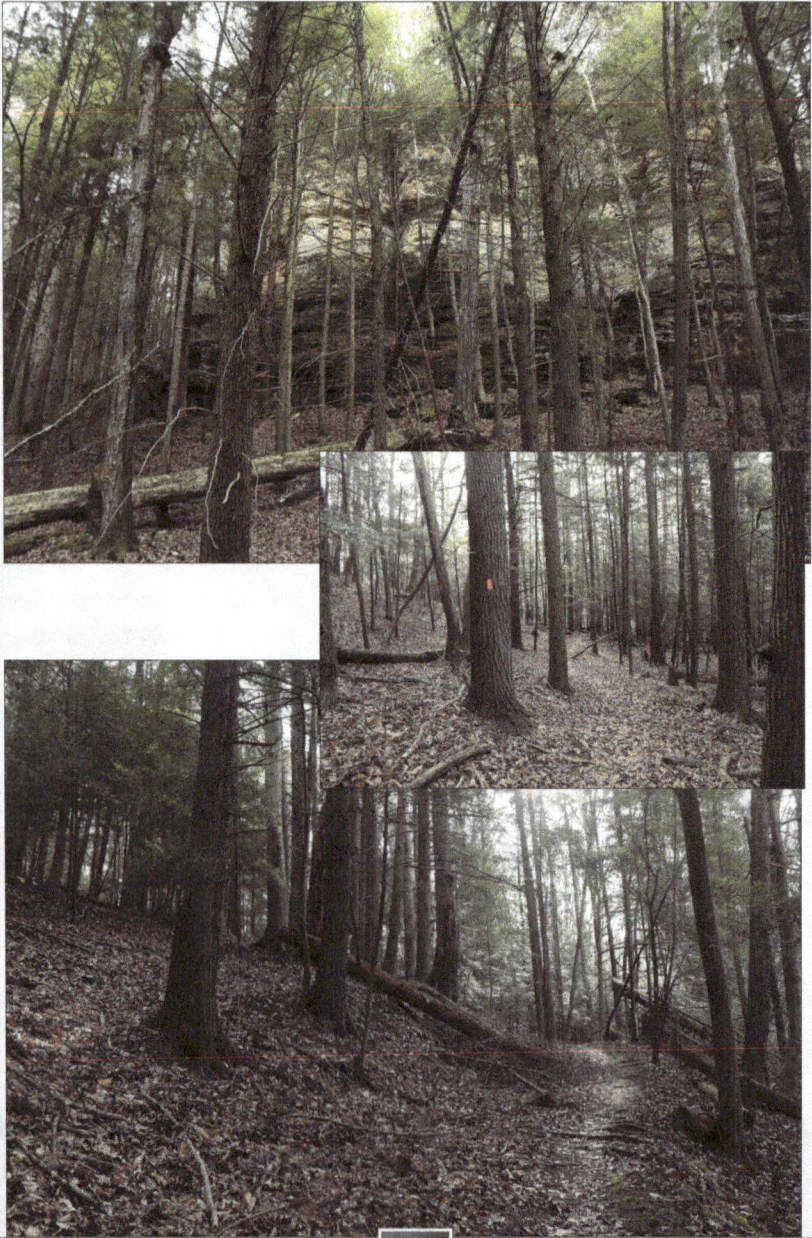

Little Rocky Hollow

State Nature Preserve

Area: Near Conkle's Hollow *Permit Only! No dogs.*

From the parking area and the trail, hikers descend to the valley through a young-growth forest and into a hemlock forest. The Buckeye Trail intersects with its well-maintained, well-blazed trail at the bottom (Little Rocky Branch) at 0.4 miles (N39° 28.786' W82° 32.480').

Hikers can choose to go left or right on the trail. The trail to the right travels through a beautiful section with creeks, many seasonal waterfalls, and rock formations. Hikers must stay on the trail. *This area is a must-see approach to exploring the Hocking Hills away from the crowds, as hiker numbers are minimal here to reduce damage to the preserve. Following the Buckeye Trail blue blazes at the bottom reduces your impact!*

Buckeye Trail Blue Blazes

A Few Challenging Routes

*Ash Cave to Cedar Falls (Hocking Hills State Park)

*Old Man's Cave to Cedar Falls (Hocking Hills State Park)

*Cemetery Ridge Trail to Hemlock Trail to Creekside Meadows Trail (Clear Creek Metro Park)

Ash Cave to Cedar Falls

(Out and Back) – 5 miles 2.0-3.0 hours Moderately challenging Parking: Ash Cave 27291 State Route 56 South Bloomingville, OH 43152 (39.395993,-82.545927)

This hike starts at Ash Cave and goes to Cedar Falls, passing the Hocking State Forest fire tower, where hikers can climb to the top for a beautiful vista view. The trail is one-way, out and back, which means hikers turn around at Cedar Falls and return on the same path. It is about 0.25 miles through Ash Cave and then 2.3 miles to Cedar Falls, a total of about 5 miles round trip.

Hikers cross State Route 56 from the parking area to the Ash Cave trailhead. After the cave, a series of steps takes hikers to the top of the waterfall, where a left heads toward the fire tower and Cedar Falls (going right will bring hikers to the parking lot and is the way out after the hike). Hikers will follow a rugged, worn dirt path until it runs into a wide old forestry service road with some rock base. A sign denotes the fire tower and is easily seen. The trail continues after the tower and through a parking lot across Chapel Ridge Road, where a dirt path continues and eventually connects with Forestry Road again. At Cedar Falls, hikers cross the parking lot roadway and continue at the entranceway, which is easy to find as it is across from the large restrooms. At Cedar Falls, the trail loops back to the parking area, where hikers can return to Ash Cave.

Map

Cedar Falls

Ash Cave Fire Tower
39°24'21.1"N 82°31'50.7"W

Ash Cave

Parking

Image: OpenStreetMap

N

Old Man's Cave to Cedar Falls

(Out and Back) 5.0 miles 2.0-3.0 hours Moderately challenging
Parking: Kiosk at Old Man's Cave Parking Lot State Route 664,
Logan OH 43138 (39.436690, -82.539316)
The Kiosk is here: (39.436380, -82.539181)

This hike starts at Old Man's Cave and goes to Cedar Falls, passing through the gorge and up into Old Man's Cave. After hikers ascend the stone steps, they pass the Old Naturalist Cabin and make a right to cross an A-frame bridge. After the bridge, hikers will turn right to follow the Gorge Overlook Trail, leading through a dense forest and past Rose Lake, crossing the dam. After crossing the dam, hikers will take a right and continue until they cross a second A-frame Bridge over Cedar Falls and follow the trail right. After descending wooden steps, Cedar Falls will be on the right. Hikers return along the same route.

Map

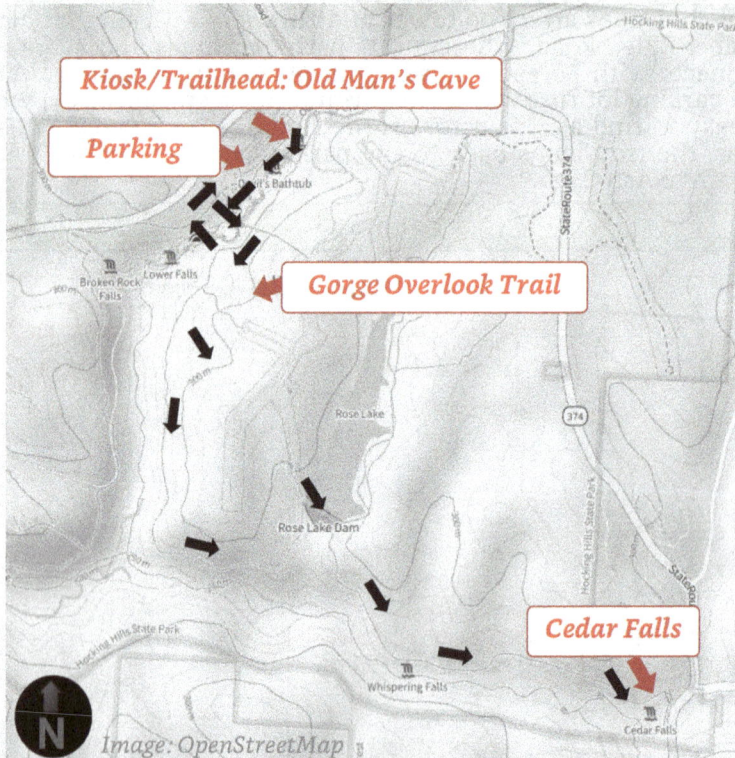

Kiosk/Trailhead: Old Man's Cave

Parking

Gorge Overlook Trail

Cedar Falls

Image: OpenStreetMap

Clear Creek Metro Park- Cemetery Ridge Trail to Hemlock Trail to Creekside Meadows

(Loop) 5.5 miles 2.0-3.0 hours Moderately challenging Parking: Creekside Meadows Picnic Area Rockbridge, OH 43149 (39.589008, -82.577634) No dogs allowed.

5.5 miles up hill and moderately strenuous on an old road within a deep forest, then along a well-used dirt path (up a hill) through a hemlock forest and beside huge and beautiful rock formations, and after following beside the babbling Clear Creek back to parking area. Some muddy patches seasonally. It is moderately strenuous. (No dogs allowed) **Park at Creekside Meadows Parking** Area. **Follow the Creekside Meadows trail near the rear of the parking area by the pit toilets 0.2 miles. Make a left at the fork which will lead toward Clear Creek Road** which hikers will cross to get to the Cemetery Ridge Trail trailhead (watch for oncoming traffic). **Follow the Cemetery Ridge Trail 2.2 miles where Chestnut Trail intersects. Turn left to continue along Cemetery Ridge trail another 0.3 miles.** There is a sign indicating **Fern Trail. Take a left where hikers immediately see a sign showing that Hemlock Trail will be in 0.3 miles. At the Hemlock Trail trailhead sign, make a left.** Follow Hemlock Trail 1.5 miles until Clear Creek Road intersects and continue straight across the road (watch for oncoming traffic) where Creekside Meadows Trail intersects. Make a left on Creekside Meadows Trail and travel 0.5 miles back to Creekside Meadows Parking Area.

Map

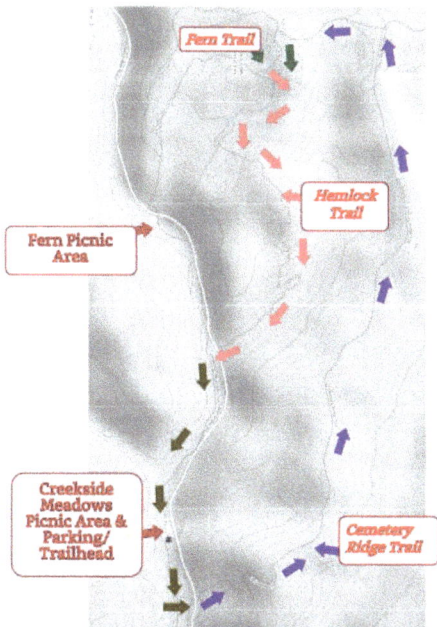

The arrow colors above match notations on park maps:
Cemetery Ridge Trail: Purple   Fern: Green
Hemlock Trail: Pink   Creekside Meadows: Brown